# Exposing**nature**

## The Natural History Museum Photography Guide

Frank Greenaway

Published by the Natural History Museum, London

First published by the Natural History Museum,
Cromwell Road, London SW7 5BD
© Natural History Museum, London, 2006

ISBN: 0 565 09193 X
ISBN 13: 978 0 565 09193 4

A catalogue record for this book is available from
the British Library.

Edited by Jonathan Elphick
Designed by Mercer Design
Reproduction and printing by Craft Print, Singapore

Cover images
Front cover: Puma (*Puma concolor*) in snow.
© Ellen Goff/NHMPL

Distribution
NBN International
Estover Road
Devon PL6 7PY
UK

# Contents

# Introduction

# Introduction

To write a book about how to succeed with nature photography is a little like telling someone how to climb a mountain. When it actually comes to it, there is nothing to beat practical experience and knowledge of one's own capabilities – and limitations. Despite this, it is possible to give a good deal of advice, both general and specific, and this guide aims to do just that. Unlike many other such books, it dwells rather more on the natural history of the subject and the photographer's approach to it than concentrating on the technical aspects.

## Know your own motivation

Natural history photography is enormously popular with individual involvement ranging from the relatively superficial to the fanatical. Whatever the degree of commitment, it is a very good idea to begin by clearly examining and understanding your motivation.

There is no need to share this personal exploration with others unless you want to, although an experienced amateur or professional may provide a good sounding board and also help you to arrive at an accurate analysis. This preliminary exercise requires absolute honesty.

Once revealed, such motivation can lead to a much more purposeful approach to the making of pictures and, even more importantly, what you do with them afterwards.

A very common example of failure in this respect comes from those photographers who set out to obtain images that meet their own personal likes and interests with little consideration of what they will do with them. Feeling confident, with a growing collection of images, the photographer then attempts to market them, usually with a picture library. Often, quite a lot of pictures are accepted, but then very few sell. To sell a large number of images consistently, one has to create them with their sales potential as the main influence, from inception to final presentation.

Merely convincing yourself of the beauty of nature by attempting to illustrate it to one's personal satisfaction and then expecting a rush of purchasers to share your enthusiasm is not a recipe for commercial success. A much more suitable outlet for this kind of work would be to exhibit beautifully made prints at the many clubs, societies and galleries that organise such displays, and to use your talent and technique towards attaining this goal.

An example of successfully blending motivation and photography is the university lecturer or teacher who requires photographic material to illustrate specific points in a presentation. Such a person knows the subject well and can tailor the images they obtain to their particular requirements.

Previous page: Exotic locations can mean exotic difficulties for the photographer. Snow creates unbelievably bright highlights, which when combined with the very dark plumage of this Adélie penguin (*Pygoscelis adeliae*) makes for an extremely tricky composition.

Left: The estate of Gallanach on the Hebridean island of Coll off the west coast of Scotland. This image is an example of a successful entrant in the internationally famous Wildlife Photographer of the Year Competition. It has great atmosphere and works well as a large display print.

# Know your subjects

Understanding the behaviour of target species should underpin any serious attempt at natural history photography in the field. The observation and recording of such behaviour has long played a role in wildlife photography and, as time has passed and equipment become more versatile, it has become more and more sophisticated. Part of the magic of prolonged observation of the natural world is that eventually very subtle clues can be recognised and understood that tell a much more detailed story than is directly obvious. It is such observations that allow the experienced birdwatcher to identify birds seen only briefly or at extreme range by their flight patterns or feeding actions. Similarly, the skilled botanist quickly recognises the wildflowers growing in a woodland even though it is midwinter and very little growth is visible above ground.

Naturalists use such clues continually and almost automatically, though unfortunately novices must resign themselves to the fact that it can take many years to acquire the necessary knowledge. It is the successful depiction of a group of such clues, summed up as a particular animal or plant's 'jizz', to use the birdwatcher's term, that frequently transforms a photograph – or a piece of artwork – from a mere representation of an animal or plant into something which has captured a little of the essence of that particular species. In skilled hands, the subject may be represented so well that a series of little dots in the background of a seascape could be recognised with certainty to species level by those in the know. Adding such small details can turn what would have otherwise been mundane images into natural history masterpieces.

It is likely that Stone Age people created their cave paintings in the belief that fixing the images of the creatures they portrayed in time and space would give them some power over the animals they hunted, and in one sense this was quite true. The portrayals, while far from technically perfect representations of the particular species of animals concerned, are instantly recognisable – even though they may be just a few marks on a cave wall.

By becoming sufficiently well acquainted with the subject matter it is possible to build this level of insight into your nature photography, and as a result to experience the joy of an entirely different level of appreciation of the efforts of others, whether artwork or photography.

Left: This pregnant lesser
horseshoe bat (*Rhinolophus
hipposideros*) was
photographed travelling along a
flight line leading from its roost.

Above: The wing and tail
patterns of waders flying in
groups can be an aid to their
specific identification, as with
these red knots (*Calidris canuta*)
over the great estuary of the
Wash in Norfolk. Capturing a
creature's 'jizz' so that it is
instantly identifiable is quite a
challenge. An added bonus is
that repeated patterns such
as these can make for very
beautiful images, especially
when they are taken with a
background of a shoreline at
dawn or sunset.

# The ethics of nature photography

The advent of the digital image presents the wildlife photographer with many more possibilities than were available before. Images have long been tailored to a rectangular format and presented that way in picture frames or publications. Photography had become very conservative in its presentation. This mould has been broken, and one nowadays often sees images as little cutouts spread through a publication or as parts of images breaking up a pattern of text.

At its simplest, the digital approach now makes it possible for home photographers to assemble a series of images into a presentation that includes text and even video clips and to express themselves in a very fluid, adaptable way. In its most complex form, it opens the door to combining some of the aspects of both artist and photographer. In the same way as it is possible to pack extra information into an image by capitalising on an understanding of animal 'jizz', it is now also possible to add multiple sets of information into a single presentation.

There has long been an ethic in nature photography that insists on the single unadulterated image. This idea springs from the requirement of scientific photography for faithful,

Altering the content of images has become a relatively easy task with the arrival of digital cameras. One of these herring gull (*Larus argentatus*) chicks has had its background altered to remove some obtrusive dark areas (left). In this instance the work is of little consequence but it could easily have introduced information from another image that totally altered the context of the original.

un-retouched representations of subjects. It is an ethic that has saved the profession from many possible misrepresentations and hoaxes, but has not entirely eliminated them. Digital manipulation gives the freedom to work with images to explore new angles that can at best transcend any results achievable by traditional methods, but at worst be a complete fiction. There is a basic difference between changing the parameters of an image and changing its content. This is well shown by recent pictures from Mars. The parameters of colour, sharpness, contrast and so on are all changed at will to wring out the last scrap of information. Pictures are joined and perspective is corrected, but the basic content remains totally unaltered.

The modern television or film spectaculars on subjects such as dinosaurs are another example: no one criticises the methods, only the accuracy or interpretation of the information portrayed. There is certainly a place for such manipulation; it is just that the material must be accurate in portrayal, representation and rendition.

When imagination plays a part it should be clear that it has done so. All such work that comes from this approach will be seen as heretical by some critics, but it is certainly an

exciting option for the future. The best exponents of these up-to-the-minute techniques will be able to combine the technology, the art and the science to the benefit of all three.

Natural history photography is a direct method of communication that has been made to work very hard over the years, usually with the altruistic intent of sharing an appreciation of the natural world and by so doing to help protect it. Nonetheless, meeting the need for recording natural events in new and exciting ways is often extremely expensive and carries with it the pressure to go to ever greater lengths to achieve that stunning still image, video sequence or film footage. The growing pace of loss of natural habitats means that the impact of visitors on those wild places that remain becomes more and more intense. Almost all nature photographers have an abiding

of film and this has led to increased visitor pressure, which some such places simply cannot sustain. The precautions necessary before embarking on photography in wild habitats should always include the need to avoid direct disturbance, but should not stop there. Indeed, it may sometimes be hard to justify going in at all, if the risks of doing harm are high. And perhaps as viewers we should temper our avid consumption of each bigger and better wildlife spectacular with caution.

Few other human activities short of habitat modification and destruction have as much potential for long-term disturbance as photography, particularly to birds and mammals. Many sites and animals in the world are repeatedly the subjects of intensive photography over many years. Even if the photographers are 'accepted' by the animals concerned who is to say that other humans will not betray this trust?

It is a prime responsibility to abide by local and national laws, rules and regulations that govern wildlife photography, and to avoid disturbing shy animals by your presence or close approach. Virtually all national governments have wildlife departments or authorities appointed for this purpose who will be very ready to give advice and when necessary issue the appropriate permits. A good rule of thumb is: 'if you would not do it at home do not do it anywhere else'.

**Left: Lions (*Panthera leo*) at Musiara Marsh, in the famous Masai Mara game reserve, Kenya. Wild animals can become habituated to the presence of humans. This can be problematic in the long term, as not all humans can be trusted to merely observe. Conditions and times can and do change and what is unthinkable one year can become the norm a year or two later. Changing national attitudes to whaling and harvesting ivory are just two examples of this.**

love of their subjects and would not wish to see them harmed in any way.

Even so, the photography of wildlife can often bring disturbance with it either directly, by the stress caused by intrusions into animals' lives, or indirectly, by exposing them to unnecessary predation by one's very presence. Huge numbers of people worldwide first became aware of the world's most popular wildlife sites through the medium

# Safe storage and retrieval of images

Every photographer likes to keep their images in good order, but inevitably few last as long as fifty years and even fewer are saved as records of their time. This is either because of failure of the image medium or a failure on the part of the photographers to produce work that has genuine appeal and is understood and appreciated beyond their own lifetime. It is certainly the case that photography is not the permanent record that many think it to be. Indeed, in many cases, the picture is more fragile than the subject itself. The quality of many pictures from even a few tens of years ago is usually abysmal, not because they were like that when created, but usually because of repeated copying or chemical decay. Often it is this chemical decay rather than the image itself that is appreciated in old work.

Preservation has not been improved by the digital capture of modern images. Such is the nature of the currently available methods of image storage that longevity is hardly an issue worth considering. Human nature is such that each individual who handles a digital image attempts to improve it, in sharpness or contrast, or in a dozen other ways. The net result of this practice is a severe loss of image quality, normally with no original to return to. The total loss of stored data due to damaged hard discs or unreadable compact discs is set to replace the faded transparency or 'eight by ten' of previous years.

All photographers should at least attempt to remedy this situation by preserving their original image data in the most permanent medium they can find.

Currently the best storage medium for digital images is the single-sided compact disc, although the discs vary greatly in quality. It is almost impossible to obtain information on their archival qualities from manufacturers. The best policy is to buy high-quality discs, to avoid reusable ones and to store them in cool and dark conditions. With valued images always archive the master file or the raw data as well as any final manipulated image. This way the original data can be referred back to if the working image becomes corrupted. In time, compact discs are sure to be replaced by new perhaps better methods. Always bear in mind that your up-to-date method of displaying your stored data is likely to become obsolete and even disappear very rapidly as technology changes, and make sure you transfer valued images to good new storage systems as they become mainstream technology.

'Tried and tested' is a good maxim for archives and it is hard to beat good old black-and-white silver prints on paper. They have lasted a hundred years in often adverse conditions and still remained fresh and useable. Apart from a very few special processes, colour images as prints will not have anywhere near this life expectancy.

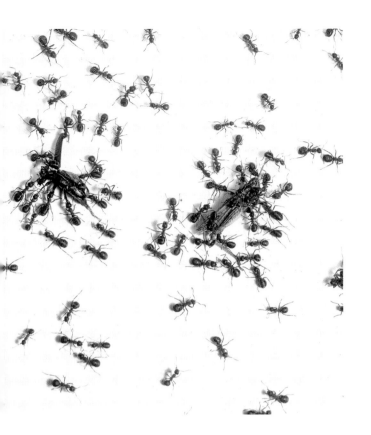

## Adapting to change

With so many possible future developments, photography is set to enhance its position as the communication medium of the future. Even in the last ten years it is noticeable how the use of photographic images has increased in almost all forms of communication. From major national newspapers to local broadsheets, it is now expected that the overview of the information will be in the images. In the field of natural history, in particular, photography is set to make big changes. While powerful traditions of style have their place in wildlife photography, the use of images in different media has demanded new styles of photography. This is clearly shown by the contrasting images of the foraging wood ants. No photographer is worth the name unless they show their best images from the best of their work available. Both the immediate nature of the medium and the possibilities it creates have changed so radically that the best in the future will be of a different order.

Above and right: Foraging wood ants, (*Formica rufa*) make regular pathways and use all sorts of techniques to overcome obstacles in their way. They also carry nest material and food back into the nest along these cleared and scent-trailed tracks. Their behaviour can be fascinating and will provide endless opportunity for close photography. One of the joys of such photography is that the subject material is readily available in the warmer months and is unlikely to be disturbed by the constant attention of a photographer.

Left: Archiving images should always be done with the original scan or digital image, before any alterations or enhancements are carried out on it. Tailoring images to a particular use often means that the scan will be altered so much that it will lose either some of its area or become overworked digitally and begin to lose detail, as with these shots of a northern wheatear (*Oenanthe oenanthe*).

# Technical aspects

# Technical aspects

To many people, the camera is a device that forever gets in the way of picture taking, while to others it is simply a tool for capturing images. But photography is really best viewed as a technical pursuit blended with an artistic approach. To do it well requires the best of both worlds: anything less is either 'record' photography or merely a technical exercise. Carefully choosing equipment for your requirements rather than solely for ease of use is a major part of success in photography.

There is essentially only one major difference between film and digital photography. This is the swapping of wet chemical processing of film images for digital image information storage on computers. However, in practice, this is a pretty fundamental difference. Many will breathe a sigh of relief at the passing of the photographic darkroom into history, for it is of course totally unnecessary in digital work. On the other hand, antique collectors specialising in old equipment may reap big rewards in years to come, as purchase prices are dropping to rock bottom. Recently, many millions of pounds' worth of

beautifully made darkroom equipment has been made virtually worthless in the space of a few years by the rapid decline of wet photographic processing.

The traditional method still has a few years to run as a significant part of the photographic industry. However, as with many other processes in the history of photography – or of any technology – most of this outdated equipment will disappear without a trace to be replaced by ever-faster computers. This state of affairs is a manufacturer's dream. Changes in the film photographic industry had become very slow as the technology had just about reached its maximum potential. As a result, the requirement for new or different equipment was low and the market had slowed down. The advent of useable digital photography has been a godsend to the industry.

We can expect to be tempted by constant offerings of ever so slightly improved camera models and associated computers for many, many years to come. This may seem like a rather cynical view, but it is a very useful one to adopt when buying equipment and attempting to avoid the sales talk and obtain the information that you really need to make your purchase last as a useable item.

Previous page: A herd of African elephants (*Loxodonta africana*) pictured against the backdrop of Mount Kilimanjaro in Amboseli National Park, Kenya.

The equipment required to photograph even one species in a range of situations can be extensive. Although both these pictures feature lesser horseshoe bats (*Rhinolophus hipposideros*), the one opposite shows an individual photographed in the field foraging for insect food and that on the left is of an adult female suckling its baby with another juvenile alongside. The field shot is a high-speed flash image where the bat has taken its own picture by breaking an infrared light beam, while the roost image was taken using a hand-held camera with an automatic hand-held flashgun and a reflector. In both cases the camera was a Rollei 6008 but the lenses were 80mm and 150mm respectively.

## Selecting equipment

Natural history photography takes many forms, and although photographers often specialise in some aspect of the craft, many are also great generalists. It would require a comprehensive assessment of all the equipment on the market to cover all the needs for natural history photography, and such a review is beyond the scope of this book. Some general understanding, at least, about how the different equipment works will provide the basis for selecting purchases to suit one's needs, aims and finances, and it is this generalised information that will be provided here. The expense of so much photographic equipment is a severe handicap to virtually all photographers, professional and amateur alike. If you know your subject and have properly thought through a project, it is relatively easy to draw up an ideal list of equipment needed. The problem is you may have a dozen very different projects in the space of a year or two. Ever ready to cash in on such enthusiasm for tackling a whole range of subjects, the manufacturers have realised this and endeavour to provide cameras that are all things to all people. In some respects they succeed, but often they have ended up with overcomplicated gadget boxes with a bewildering range of controls.

## Film or digital?

When considering new equipment that has to satisfy your different needs, there are some basic decisions that will rule out many items. It is not a good idea to buy a film-only camera, as it seems inevitable that film will rise in price rapidly as the mass market for it disappears. It will also become more difficult to obtain processing in any reasonable time period. An exception to this is with the medium-format cameras, such as those made by Hasselblad or Rolleiflex, that will accept digital backs in place of their previous film backs, giving them a total flexibility not currently found with 35mm film cameras. The renowned medium-format cameras offered by these two famous manufacturers are expensive professional (and heavy) items offering in the digital back very large megapixel counts (over 20 megapixels) and consequently large image file sizes. They give an ability to crop a section of an image to a smaller size with some of the facility offered by film. The best aspect of the current 35mm film camera ranges is that with most you can buy a new digital body that will accept your existing range of film camera lenses, saving you the great expense of having to buy these expensive items again. Remember, however, that the camera 'chip' on many camera bodies is smaller than the film it replaces so all your lenses will effectively become more telephoto (or less wide-angle).

## Digital imaging

The maximum size of sharp print that a digital camera can make is governed by the number of data points (pixels) that make up the image. The light-receiving screen or 'chip' that replaces film in a digital camera is made up of a vast array of these tiny light-sensitive pixels. The size of the screen and the proximity of the pixels to each other give us a number for each camera. This is stated as a figure for each camera in megapixels. A small camera will have about four megapixels and a very large one up to 22 megapixels.

The light-receiving chips are very difficult things to manufacture, and as a result the greater the number of megapixels they contain, the higher the price tag. When you press the shutter on a digital camera, each pixel in the array receives a differing amount and colour of the light that will form a tiny portion of the image. Across the chip are groups of three adjacent pixels, each separately filtered to produce red, green and blue image data. When electronically recombined, these make a full colour image. The colour and

the intensity of the light affect the electrical charge on the pixel at the moment of exposure and this is recorded onto a memory device from each and every pixel across the chip. The result is a staggering four million individual bits of information from the smallest cameras and over twenty million from medium-format ones.

Most single-lens reflex cameras allow the user to select the quality of the saved image. This is important as it affects how many images the camera can store and at what quality. A large uncompressed image file means high picture-quality and a small one progressively lower quality. Programming the camera to save images as compressed files (most commonly those known as JPEG files) will vastly increase the number of images that can be stored in the camera. Once captured, each image is stored on a memory storage card or small micro-drive normally housed within the camera. These items are removable and it is possible to buy cards or micro-drives in a range of capacities. Be warned, however, that they are expensive and require care in handling.

Programs built into the camera adjust each image to an ideal saturation and contrast as created by the manufacturers. With some cameras it is possible to alter this program or even to access the raw data itself. If you are a computer buff this can be a very productive way of controlling the look of your final image to your own satisfaction.

## Film imaging

Film is a complicated multi-layered material. It has a support layer, usually made of a plastic that becomes clear after processing. On top of this is a coat consisting of up to seven different layers of gelatine, each laden with light-sensitive silver salts. Various chemical and physical methods are used to increase or change the light and colour sensitivity of the layers. Three basic layers are red-, green-, and blue-sensitive to produce a colour image; the others are normally there to control contrast, to prevent the film from curling up, and to avoid problems with the dyes that create the final image. Increasing the size of the silver salt crystals makes possible increases in the light sensitivity of the film, but also leads to the image being broken up by the relatively large size of the silver salt grains. When the film is exposed, tiny specks of pure silver form on the silver salt crystals. These remain unchanged until the film is processed. Different processing systems can allow either negatives or positives to be produced. During processing, dipping the film in chemical baths has the two functions of greatly enlarging the tiny silver specks to create a silver image and of activating colour dyes at these sites of development. The silver is then bleached away to leave a colour dye-negative image. Knowing even this simple sketch of the basic features helps one appreciate that photographic film is an extraordinary feat of chemical engineering.

## Light sensitivity with a digital and film methods

Film manufacturers make their products with a range of sensitivity to light. The 'film speed' is indicated by the rating given on the packet. A slow film (that is, the least sensitive) will have a rating of 50 and the fastest (most sensitive) up to 800 or beyond. In practice, slow films have terrific colour saturation, sometimes too high, and a very fine image quality. As the film speed rises, the saturation lowers and the image quality begins to fail.

Digital cameras allow the photographer to set the light sensitivity of the chip. The only really troublesome problem caused by setting the chip sensitivity, or ISO number, at a high level is the generation of 'noise' in the image. This noise is the random triggering of individual pixels that have actually not received any light. It causes a random scatter of bright dots across the image. Long exposures on digital cameras can cause the same 'noise' effect.

## The choice of camera

The range of facilities offered by most modern cameras, whether film or digital, is staggering, but then so are the expectations and requirements of many budding natural history photographers. Matching a camera to a particular specialist interest is not that difficult, but finding a model suitable for the entire area of natural history photography certainly is. Most photographers end up with several cameras which they use according to the requirements of the job in hand.

It is difficult to recommend specific makes and models as facilities, quality and price all overlap, complicating the issue, and the pace of change is so fast, with new models being brought out constantly. It is, however, possible to list some of the requirements for the major types of natural history photography (see box p.23). On the other hand, some very specialised areas, such as high-speed photography, specialised laboratory work or underwater photography require equally specialised equipment; this may have to be

assembled or even made by the photographer for a specific task. A range of examples of such special needs are described in the text under the headings of the different types of nature photography.

Camera choice is not the only factor determining how an image will turn out. These two very different action shots of a springbok (*Antidorcas marsupialis*) were taken by the same photographer using the same camera and film. The dramatic contrast in style is achieved merely by changing the shutter speed. The mid-air image showing the springbok leaping or 'pronking' was taken using a fast shutter speed – in this case 1/1500th of a second. This has enabled the photographer to maintain a sharp image. In contrast, with the motion shot of the running springbok, the shutter speed was slowed down to 1/30th of a second. This causes the blurred effect, which captures a sense of the animal's speed.

Opposite: This image of little terns (*Sterna albifrons*) was made from a hide slowly moved in close to the nest site. To take full advantage of the static position within a hide, medium format cameras are the perfect choice. Cost with digital medium format is, however, quite prohibitive. Should you wish to use a single lens reflex and telephoto lens from a hide do make sure the lens has its own central tripod mount, otherwise excessive strain will result on the camera body.

Left: A camera that is light enough to be carried around for long periods, robust enough to stand the odd knock and capable of producing an image suitable for lecture purposes are common requirements for nature photography. Many digital single lens reflex cameras will suit these needs, as used here to photograph a common sandpiper chick (*Actitis hypoleucos*).

# Possible camera/lens requirements for different kinds of bird and mammal photography

## Stalking birds or mammals

- Single-lens reflex camera body
- Choice of auto-exposure modes/manual override
- Reasonably light in weight
- Motor drive
- Largest affordable chip size and mega pixel count
- Quiet in use
- External flash synchronisation socket
- Flash exposure compensation
- Longer telephoto lenses with autofocus/manual override and tripod mount
- Lenses should focus sufficiently close to allow a sparrow to fill the frame

## For pictures obtained at feeders, earths, dens or from hides

- Single-lens reflex camera body
- External flash synchronisation socket
- Flash exposure compensation
- Choice of auto-exposure mode with manual override
- Largest affordable chip size and megapixel count
- Mirror lock

- Remote control socket for a long lead or radio release
- Long battery life in cold conditions
- Quiet in use
- Fast shutter response
- Standard focal length lens with autofocus/manual override to at least 0.5 m
- Short telephoto or 35-150mm zoom with autofocus/manual override
- Sturdy tripod with efficient quick-release fitting

## General close-up photography

- Single-lens reflex camera body
- Choice of auto-exposure mode with manual override
- Through the lens auto-flash exposure metering or manual control
- Quiet operation
- Fast shutter response
- Motor drive
- External flash synchronisation socket
- Two macro lenses (120mm and 35mm) focusing to at least x1 magnification

By not trying to get more from a small digital camera than it is really designed to achieve it is possible to concentrate on what it does really well – providing fast, moderately detailed views and close-ups. Telephoto images are the forte of the high-end single-lens reflex camera.

# Getting the most out of compact digital cameras

The major restriction with the mainstream run of famous-name single-lens reflex digital cameras is the inability to accomplish image cropping. With chips of between 6 and 12 megapixels, they simply do not have enough data points to allow major cropping and maintain quality. This dilemma necessitates a whole new approach to framing an image.

After a lifetime of selecting cropped portions of images, many photographers find it very difficult with a digital camera to get closer to their subjects and obtain the required image size in the first instance. The full frame of a modern digital reflex is usually enough for most purposes. It is, however, not the case with the smaller megapixel models. Part of the reason why the range of mini digital cameras is so popular with natural history photographers is that they can avoid the complications or impossibility of re-shooting that occurs with film. This can make it easier to ignore the disadvantages of the small file size and lack of cropping possibilities. It is inevitable that megapixel counts will continue to increase as manufacturers improve their processes. In time we can expect the current tiny cameras to have megapixel counts that rival current top-of-the-range models with all the advantages of final reproduction size or image cropping.

The small size of the digital 'chip' means that the normal lens for the camera is also a very short focal length and this in turn means that it becomes much easier to obtain focus across the entire depth of the image. The images are easy to take and sharp in depth but unfortunately do have not enough data points to make large prints before the image 'pixelates' – breaks up and shows its individual pixels. This failing should not be allowed to detract from the types of photography that these cameras excel at – small images for illustration or record.

When starting out with a small digital camera it is a good idea to sit and play with the controls until you have a solid grasp of the camera functions. You should be able to operate the menu system almost in the dark and know, without looking, just what your camera will or will not do. For the most part, natural history subjects do not wait while you consult the handbook. An encouraging fact is that people who never bothered with photography in the past have taken to these little cameras and will use them in ways that they would never have attempted with film. Mixed light sources or dark conditions are no barrier. The fact that the success or failure of the image can be monitored at the time of taking the picture seems to be the key to this popularity. It should perhaps be emphasised that digital cameras in no way alter the amount of care required to produce really good images. All the thought and effort necessary for the production of film images is required in equal amount, but with slightly different emphasis, for digital images.

If you wear spectacles for close work it is worth remembering that you will need them to view the image screen on the back of your digital camera, unlike the corrected viewfinder of a traditional camera. It can be a nuisance if you are in the field, especially under hot damp conditions where glasses are likely to mist up.

When choosing a digital camera, a prime consideration is to decide on the chief purpose to which it will be put. As indicated above, the decision will have determined the number of megapixels you require from the receiving chip and the type of accessories such as lenses that you may need. It will also have a big effect on the price. In many instances, nothing more than small prints and occasional images for lectures or other presentations may be required, and for these the lower-priced, 4-8 megapixel cameras will be light and flexible enough. Most of these little cameras have fixed zoom lenses, often with a special close-up

function, and are currently available at prices ranging from £100 to £500-plus. Be aware that the more expensive models often sport an impressive extra array of functions that you will never want to use – or even remember how to use! The beauty of these little cameras is that they do a job fast and well and with useable results on a small scale. Don't spoil what they are good at by trying to get them to do something they are poor at.

The range of digital cameras available starts with tiny, very effective models that will handle almost anything apart from taking large telephoto shots. They will, however, never make a decent print at any respectable size as they have only about four megapixels of data available for each image. Moving on to the next stage, we have the single-lens reflex models, with many more megapixels; however, even with these, about A4 size is the maximum that most will print to at the best quality. Currently, it is only the medium-format digital backs and some of the full-frame 35mm models that will capture sufficient data to make it worthwhile to produce really large prints, or allow major image cropping while maintaining maximum quality.

Any requirement for big telephoto lenses for wildlife work requires a camera with a single-lens reflex body. Usually this means more megapixels, as well as being larger, heavier and with a more expensive price tag, even before you buy the lens. Such camera bodies currently cost £600 to £2000-plus. Virtually all the famous camera manufacturers have various models available and frequently add a new one to the range.

## Negative size – chip size

Current film sizes for easily portable cameras are 35mm or 6 x 6 cm. This means that what is considered a standard lens on 35mm format (50mm focal length lens) would function as a wide-angle one on 6 x 6 cm format, because the actual film area is bigger and records information from a larger area than a 35mm frame. A standard lens on 6 x 6 cm format (80mm focal length lens) would be a small telephoto on 35mm format for the same reasons.

In fact, this trick is impossible, as the different lens mounts would not permit this interchange of lenses between formats, but the principle is important as an analogy when working with digital cameras with their differing chip sizes. The light-receiving chips in most single-lens reflex digital cameras are much smaller than the 35mm film size. As a result, the lens that was a 'standard' lens on 35mm film format now becomes a short telephoto on a digital camera. As most single-lens reflex digital bodies accept the range of lenses made by the relevant camera manufacturer for its film models, this becomes an important feature to remember. It now seems probable that future cameras will mostly be single-lens reflex models having larger or even full-frame 35mm chips. Such cameras are already available.

Should you envisage ever wanting to become involved in remotely operated photography, even just with a very long cable release, ensure that your intended camera body has a connection for this. Many modern cameras do not have one.

## Lenses for natural history photography

With virtually all compact cameras, it is not possible to fit different lenses. Instead, such models have permanently fixed small zoom lenses. So if you are considering buying one, check carefully beforehand that it will be capable of taking good pictures of your intended range of subject matter.

Features such as the range of close-up magnification available, the widest angle of view for landscapes or the longest telephoto may be important for what you aim to do. If your requirement is not met by these smaller cameras you will have to move up to the more sophisticated – and expensive – single-lens reflex models with their range of interchangeable lenses.

Each manufacturer tends to have their own lens mounting system, although some signs of standardisation are beginning to appear. The most common lens mount in general use is the Nikon bayonet fitting. Some manufacturers produce lenses designed to fit a wide range of camera makes. These are usually cheaper than the branded products but need to be tried out very carefully on the intended host body as they will not always allow the full range of camera functions to be used. Do not necessarily rule them out, though, as they are often of high optical quality.

Lens design has changed radically over the last ten years or so. This has been partly because of the desire for lighter, more automated equipment, but also because the widespread change to digital photography has allowed a greater control of the image after capture. Problems with lenses in the past have been excessive weight, slow operation and low contrast or lack of definition, especially with the zoom objectives. Weight has been lowered by the use of plastics in construction, even for the internal objective lenses themselves.

## Using autofocus systems

Autofocus technology has cured a lot of problems resulting from slow operation but created a few new ones. It pays to know exactly how your particular autofocus system works if you intend to photograph animals. Most autofocus lenses now use optical methods of range-finding, but beware of those that use pulses of infrared light or emit ultrasound from the camera. These systems can cause the camera to focus on any glass between you and your subject, such as a window. The few ultrasound types available may well scare a living wildlife subject away altogether.

The latest longer autofocus telephoto lenses are a joy to use – provided you keep a close eye on the actual focus point that the camera is giving you, for it may choose a point ever so slightly away from the optimum. This problem of the camera choosing the wrong point of focus can also occur with close-up (or 'macro') subjects, such as insects, and if this is the case, it is a good idea to flip the switch and use manual focusing for such shots. Autofocus really comes into its own when photographing the sudden appearance of an animal. Subjects such as a whale surfacing are classic examples.

## Predictive autofocus

Predictive autofocus monitors the changing position of the subject and predicts where the subject will be for the next exposure. The combination copes reasonably well with flying birds or other fast-moving subjects, provided they are a reasonable size in the image. You may find it easier, though, to use manual focus for such shots as it can be easier to concentrate on the changing image while tracking the focus.

In the past, telephoto lenses only ever performed well at small apertures, but with the digital control of contrast and sharpening now available, they are at last usable at wide apertures and in most light conditions. Zoom lenses that cover a wide range of focal length are not a good choice for natural history photography because in using one lens to do the job of several different ones, the physical laws of optics become pushed to the limit and the quality of the image suffers.

Three lenses will cover most situations and should not be excessively heavy to carry. These are a wide-angle lens, a short telephoto lens and a long telephoto one. The wide-angle lens should allow macro (close-up) work. If expense is a problem, the one to leave out is the long telephoto – unless you are particularly interested in bird or large mammal photography where it is necessary to maintain a discrete distance, either for safety or to avoid disturbance.

Really close-up photography will require the use of specialist macro lenses and perhaps even extension tubes in order to obtain sharp images in magnifications above x1. Extension tubes fit between the camera body and the lens and allow the lens to focus much closer than it would otherwise do.

## Aperture, depth of field and focal length of lenses

The diaphragm (or iris) of a lens is the multi-bladed mechanism that controls the amount of light that can pass through a lens. The variable diameter of the opening that results as the diaphragm is opened or closed is called the aperture. The aperture not only affects the amount of light that will reach the film or digital chip, but also the depth of field, or the amount of the image that will be rendered sharp. With wide apertures a narrow area on either side of the point of focus will be sharp. In practice, at distances greater than about eight times the focal length of the lens being used, this area extends one-third in front and two-thirds behind the point of critical focus. Closer than this, the area rendered sharp is more or less equidistant in front and behind the subject. As you close the diaphragm on any lens, the area of sharp focus increases and continues to increase until the lens is closed to its maximum. With very small apertures on some lenses the lens performance may begin to fall off again at the lowest settings, but for the most part this failing can be ignored.

The basic principles outlined above apply to all camera lenses. However, there are practical differences between wide-angle and telephoto lenses where depth of field is concerned. If a picture is taken of an object with a telephoto lens and a wide-angle lens with both lenses set at the same aperture and giving images at the same magnification, the depth of field will be the same for both lenses at the plane of the object. But the backgrounds and foregrounds of the images from the two lenses will be rendered at very different magnifications. The result is that the apparent depth of field that can be rendered by a wide-angle lens is much greater than that which can be rendered by a telephoto lens with the point of focus at the same magnification. This apparent increase in the obtainable depth of field from wide-angle lenses is of great practical importance in close-up photography or any work involving a requirement for extreme depth of field.

## Lens hoods and protective filters

Always use a lens hood. Not only will this shade the whole lens from stray light and increase image contrast, but it will also protect the front objective lens from twigs, scratches and even accidental falls. Besides these image improvement and protective functions, lens hoods reduce the possibility of detection by a wary subject. Animals are never at ease when faced by the 'eye' of a camera at the best of times and the reflection from the front of a large, unhooded telephoto lens is often the final straw that makes them run.

The addition of an ultraviolet- (UV-) absorbing glass filter over the front element has also protected many a lens from dust, dirt and the occasional knock. Besides this function, the chief purpose of UV filters is to correct the colour of images taken in high UV conditions. Ultraviolet light causes a blue haze in the distance that is particularly noticeable at high altitude, on snow, in the tropics or by the sea. The use of this filter will reduce the haze and allow distant detail to be rendered more clearly. UV filters can normally be left on lenses all the time.

Opposite: Often, the choice of camera lens for a particular subject is based on the expected or preferred working distance between the photographer and the subject. Unfortunately, this does not take into account the desired perspective or depth of field in the image. The images of this Harris's hawk (*Parabuteo unicinctus harrisi*) are basically at the same magnification, the same point of focus, and same depth of field, but the working distances are very different: less than 1 m (3 ft) for the wide-angle lens (top) and over 10 m (30 ft) for the telephoto lens (bottom). The perspective differs, from sufficiently wide to allow a considerable sweep of countryside to be clearly recognisable in the background and create some exaggerated foreshortening on the falconer's forearm. In comparison, the telephoto lens creates a distinctly flattened perspective and contrast, enlarging a small section of the tree branches to give only a little information about the surrounding habitat. In the originals it is also noticeable that the contrast and colour balance differ between the two images.

Above and below: Skylight filters and polarising filters lower haze in images and give clarity and saturation to distant horizons. Polarising filters in particular will allow the near elimination of reflections off water surfaces or glass.

# Shutters and shutter speeds

There are two basic types of camera shutters (although the means to power both can be either electrical or mechanical). These two types are called 'focal plane shutters' and 'between-the-lens' shutters. Both the names are usefully descriptive, as they refer to the locations of the shutters within the camera although the between-the-lens shutters are also known as 'leaf shutters' because of the shape of the individual shutter blades.

Between-the-lens shutters are devices with black metal or carbon fibre blades that block the passage of light through the centre of the lens. They are placed at the position within the lens where the light is collected into a narrow column and the shutter blades have to move a minimal amount to allow a brief exposure. The time that the shutter is open is the actual speed that is set on the camera. The fastest commercial models allow exposures of 1/1000th of a second. This may be close to the practical limits for electro-mechanical shutters as the shutter blades begin to bend when subjected to faster speeds. Electronic flash can be synchronised to any shutter speed setting with between-the-lens shutters, making them ideal equipment for flash photography of rapid events. These shutters are normally found in more expensive medium-format cameras or in cheaper film and digital cameras without reflex viewing.

Focal-plane shutters are found in almost all single-lens reflex cameras. This type of shutter works by means of a blind with a slit in it that travels across the film plane. The blind travels at a constant speed no matter what the speed setting on the camera, and the width of the slit is varied to match the camera speed setting. The result of this mechanism is that total exposures with this type of shutter can never be shorter than the travel time of the blind. This is usually 1/125th of a second for shutters that travel the long horizontal distance, but sometimes as fast as 1/250th of a second for shutters that travel vertically. Up to this speed, the slot in the blind uncovers the film and is then braked until the exposure time is up. If the shutter speed setting is increased beyond 1/250th of a second, the slit in the blind becomes progressively narrower, and any one point on the film or chip sees progressively less light – although the slit still takes 1/250th of a second to travel. With this method, the light reaching the film is equivalent to the set shutter speed, but the actual physical length of time over which the exposure is made never exceeds the 1/250th of a second travel time. Some cameras with focal plane shutters have even shorter shutter settings, down to as little as 1/3000th of a second, but they still take 1/250th of a second to achieve them.

The focal-plane system is fine until you want to use flash. Synchronising flash light can be achieved only when the width of the slit in the blind is equal to, or wider than, the width of the film or chip. If it is not, the short pulse of light from the flash will expose only the little strip of film that happens to be uncovered by the slit at the moment of the flash. These complications mean that the use of flash is limited to shutter speeds below 1/250th of a second. For most purposes this is not a problem, but occasionally it can be a nuisance. A good example is when using the amazingly fast pulse of light from a flashgun to freeze the motion of a subject. If the subject is in a dark location there will be no problem. The available daylight will be so much darker than the flash that the film or chip will simply fail to register it at the speed setting of 1/250th of a second, and the only image recorded will be the sharp image from the flash light. However, if the subject is in bright daylight, a combination exposure will result with a sharp image from the flash and a blurred image from the longer daylight exposure, one recorded on top of the other.

To obtain exposures shorter than the above with either of these two shutter types, it is possible to synchronise extremely short bright flashes of light with the open shutter under dark ambient light conditions. In this way it is possible to obtain exposures as short as 1 microsecond (one-millionth of a second). In practice, however, it is very difficult to obtain the necessary high-speed flash equipment for the job. High-speed flash guns operate at such high voltages that they are potentially dangerous in use, so manufacturers have avoided possible injury to customers by making slower, lower-voltage guns. Most photographers have to compromise, and use readily available automatic flash guns that shorten the speed of the flash in order to reduce the exposure. The majority of these automatic flashguns have a power setting that allows a fixed setting at the lowest power. The flash of light from these guns at this setting is brief and will stop a lot of action, but is also of very low intensity requiring wide lens apertures for correct exposure.

# Flash equipment

Like many other items of photographic equipment, flash gear seems to have been designed specifically to operate indoors in clean, dry surroundings. All too often, it is likely to fail out in the field in damp weather – let alone in such tricky sites as a deep cave with water dripping down or close to a great waterfall.

On the whole, compact cameras with built-in flash guns are immune to these failings. By contrast, any camera with a flash synchronisation socket for attachment of a separate flash gun will be highly susceptible to at least occasional faults. It is surprising how manufacturers have kept on using such a relatively poor contact system for sixty years. Furthermore, it is almost impossible to buy electrical leads with gold contacts to attempt to overcome the problem. Cans of WD40 lubricant are not really a solution. Hot-shoe connectors are little better and do not allow easy connection to a remote flash. On top of this there is the infuriating problem of frequent failure of slave flash systems in outdoor conditions and far-too-small battery packs. As a result, some photographers rig up their own equipment.

If you want to use flash equipment extensively in the field, you should buy equipment with external power leads. Flashguns are hungry for power and even just left turned on, most will have dead batteries within an hour or two. The external power lead will allow much larger batteries to be used that will, if necessary, drive the units for periods of days, rather than hours, at a time. Units that shut down automatically after a pre-set period are also something to avoid in any work involving low temperatures or longer periods of use during a single session. It is all too easy to imagine the situation with such devices where you have the camera and flash all ready but your subject will

not co-operate. After a ten minute wait it suddenly springs to life and you press the shutter release, only to discover that the flash has automatically shut down because it was not used within five minutes.

Most close-up (macro) photography can be improved by the use of flash. Faster shutter speeds and tiny apertures together with crisp lighting get over most macro problems. Ringflash systems are particularly suitable, and you can include a small slave flash as a backlight. Such systems are often accused of producing flat-looking lighting but this is really only true of ringflash used at rather longer distances; when used in close-up they can produce startlingly good results. Modelling – the careful positioning of lights to show the three-dimensional nature of an object – can be improved somewhat if the results look a little flat by placing a diffuser of tissue paper over the right-hand top side of the flash tube. If you are photographing subjects at night, consider a ringflash unit with an on-board white light to focus by, as this system makes life much easier. Within the constraints outlined above, the ringflash and slave backlight combination is ideal equipment for the fast, consistent close-up work often required by the naturalist.

Flash lighting of large areas at night requires planning and usually setting things up in daylight – perhaps days beforehand – for shy animals. The equipment will have to endure low temperatures as well as rain, damp and perhaps even snow. It is difficult to recommend any equipment for such purposes as most of it will eventually fail under such conditions. To succeed with such photography you must become your own electrical engineer and modify, waterproof and generally tinker with your equipment until a suitable system is up and running.

## Tripods

Whatever benefits all the recent advances in camera equipment design have brought to the nature photographer, none has as yet solved the need for tripods in situations that require long exposures or the use of big telephoto lenses. Always awkward to carry and frequently excessively heavy, they can turn photography from a pleasure into an endurance test. Many photographers will have suffered the pain of fingers crushed between closing legs of tripods that seem to have minds of their own.

Thankfully, modern materials have come to the aid of those who actually hate tripods, useful though they certainly are. Modern carbon-fibre models are at least light in weight if rather expensive. Some well-known nature photographers admit to owning about ten different ones of nearly as many different sorts, because of their interest in using automated exposure where each set-up may require as many as six tripods to support all the cameras, flashguns, infra-red curtains, and so on. Carrying that lot over a few miles of mountain terrain is enough to put anyone off nature photography for life. A neat solution is to copy various established photographers by resorting to a two- wheeled trolley to move the whole lot in one go.

Whatever the problems of transporting tripods, they repay the effort in sharper images. Any scenic image has more atmosphere when lit by natural light and frequently this will mean long exposures. The required depth of field for an image may also cause exposures to lengthen. No matter what your camera, any exposure longer than about 1/30th of a second needs the camera on a solid base to hold it steady. Sometimes just resting your camera on a rock or fence post will do but this will limit your choice of camera positions, which is never a good idea. The unfortunate truth is that carrying a tripod is the answer to these problems.

One of the specialist requirements of natural history photography is a tripod that will support a camera right down to ground level. Many models available today are designed to work in studios at waist height, so look very carefully at your requirement and what your proposed purchase will actually do.

Repeat images taken by hand at one location will always have slightly different framing from image to image. This can be highly distracting when a series is presented on screen. The only way to obtain consistent frame boundaries is to mount the camera on a firmly locked-down tripod base.

## Storage bags/cases/backpacks

Small compact cameras are very robust and often need little more than a soft bag to keep dust and dirt off them. Many will fit comfortably in a pocket. Be warned, from these humble beginnings camera bags can only grow. Big may seem wonderful as you are packing up your gear for a trip. It becomes much less so after you have carried the resulting bulky, heavy bag, case or backpack for a while. Points to consider are:

- Size and loaded weight

- What you need to protect your equipment from

- Portability

You may need to tailor the bag, case or backpack to the job in hand. For example, for a trip down a cave to photograph bats, you could take a foam-lined metal-shelled case that can double as a set of steps to take pictures of hibernating bats high up on the walls. Although a bit on the heavy side, it is mostly gritproof and waterproof.

For normal photographic work above ground, you can use a relatively small soft fabric case that can be opened and closed quietly and has room for a complete medium-format camera together with flash kit attached as a single 'ready for use' macrophotography item, or a camera with a substantial telephoto lens mounted for instant long-distance shots.

More complicated set-ups in the field may require as many as six tripods and at least three cases of kit all tied on to a wheeled trolley. It is unwise to contemplate carrying this amount of gear without lots of pre-planning and observational field work, to make sure that capturing the event one is after is a probability, rather than a possibility. All overseas trips require substantial flight cases for relatively large amounts of gear – as well as good insurance.

Anybody considering serious field work will need to consider camouflage for their bags and equipment. These days, this needs to be considered with great care as anything camouflaged is immediately considered to be military equipment by officialdom. This can have serious repercussions when overseas. Camouflage applied to equipment will also seriously lower its value. The normal answer to these problems is to use camouflaged lightweight soft cloths to cover equipment in use, and have dull coloured camera bags for most other occasions.

# Digital projectors

Many nature photographers wish to produce projectable images for lectures and other presentations. Conventional slide projectors are rapidly disappearing from lecture theatres and presentations using this medium are frequently regarded as old-fashioned. Digital projectors are coming down in price, but are still likely to cost more than a mid-range digital camera, and in addition you have to have a laptop computer to run the system. The image quality of most digital projectors is poor by comparison with the best image thrown by top-quality film projectors and slides. The light sources in digital projectors have lives limited to 2000 to 3000 hours and are very expensive to replace, so they are not the sort of item to leave running while you sort out which images to use. However, even with these drawbacks, the flexibility of presentation offered by the digital alternative is a huge advantage, making it simple to produce text overlays and changes in the style of images. On the other hand, though, the possibilities of disaster during a digital projector presentation must not be forgotten, and it is always necessary to check that your images are actually compatible with the projector well before any public presentation.

# Composition, style and collections

Creating order and balance in an image is a very personal thing. Any rules of composition need to be infinitely flexible, as this aspect is an essential part of the continuing appeal of photography that keeps it forever fresh and changing. Constantly and systematically applying the established tenets of composition without personal interpretation can produce competent but lifeless images. The rules are simply generally agreed guidelines for producing an image arrangement that most people will find pleasing.

A centre of interest located at the point of intersecting thirds, the point where lines drawn across from one-third of the height and one-third of the width meet, is perhaps the one commonly accepted principle worth remembering. This area allows a powerful picture element to be used without dominating or unbalancing the rest of the image rectangle. Such useful principles may be relatively loose in interpretation and application, but are taken extremely seriously by designers in many fields beyond photography and the art world. In the urge to create order in other forms of design we find exactly the same force as that involved in producing images that conform to basic rules. Try and live with an unsympathetic composition prominently displayed in your home and you will soon come to see just how important this is.

Looking for and recording order, pattern, symmetry and form in the natural world continues to play an enormously important part in successful natural history photography. Unfortunately, this is an area that, once understood, can lose much of its charm, and many such images may seem repetitive to the experienced photographer. Pattern and structure are inextricably woven into natural objects. When composing images to emphasise this aspect of their beauty, extreme care over composition and subtlety of representation generally produces more pleasing results than the imposition of strict rules.

Previous page: Graphic images are best kept simple, as with this Yucca plant photographed on the dunes of White Sands National Monument in New Mexico.

Small changes to the cropping of an image can greatly alter its impact. These two reproductions of a great cormorant (*Phalacrocorax carbo*) are taken from a single image cropped for different purposes: firstly, for its natural history interest (opposite); secondly, as a graphic exercise in pattern for a book chapter opener (below). A vertical crop of the image would have been decidedly unsympathetic to the subject.

# A personal style

Composition is one of the fundamental ingredients of that intangible group of elements that create a personal style. It does not pay to work hard at achieving a definite style; generally, it seems to grow with time and without conscious effort. It is of course you the photographer, by your choice of viewpoint, equipment, lighting and so on, who is in control of a final result. If you feel that you are not in total control of all these aspects you have not yet reached a stage when your own individual style can form. Many modern cameras, however, are so automated that they can create what amounts to a style of their own. Photography though is all about differing viewpoints, mental as well as photographic.

For the semi-professional an individual style is actually extremely difficult to maintain when one's work is published or offered for sale from agency sources. Designers working on page layouts who commission pictures direct from photographers can brief them carefully and obtain exactly the images they want, composed to fit the layout and brief. When images are obtained from agencies they will rarely be ideal in terms of layout, and designers often crop and cut the available material, regardless of the photographers' original ideas – or indeed of what the image can stand.

Thankfully, the advent of the digital age means that if you buy an image from an agency nowadays, it has already been scanned, so the range of cropping open to the layout designer is limited by the size of the scan. If you want to sell your work via agencies it is worth remembering that publishers are very conservative when it comes to composition. They like simple images with the main interest very large, as this will enable them to be reproduced at any page size. If you want to sell your images, keep both them and the composition simple.

Simple images help sell pictures. These two of a dew-covered spider's web and the underside of flowers (family Asteraceae) were taken in Wiltshire, UK. Both images will allow a range of cropping to suit different reproduction formats without losing too much of the integrity of the original.

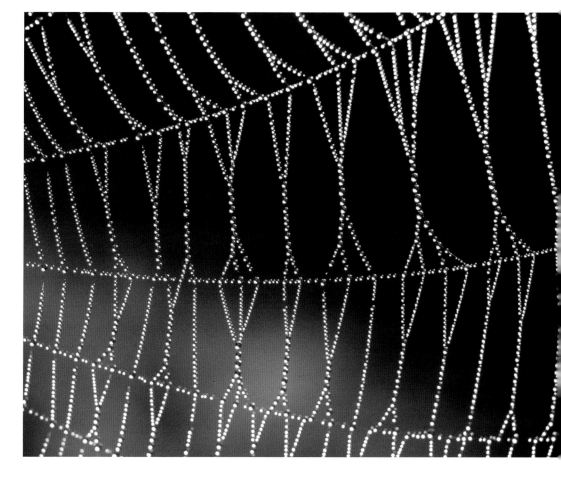

# Image size

The final size of an image has a massive influence on just what is possible in terms of content. Unfortunately for photographers, the reproduction size of their work in many books is often far too small to show the detail that the images were originally framed to reveal. Since printed images may be little bigger than postage stamps, the original shot must be bold and simple because any detail will simply be too small to interpret. Increasing size means that more and more detail becomes visible and images can become more complex. A limit is reached when you cannot view the whole image without turning your head. By this stage the actual image structure is normally breaking down into pixels or film grain, and further magnification reveals nothing.

Size is an integral part of image visualisation and should be considered from the beginning of the process of thinking about creating a possible image. A classic illustration of this is the landscape image. By the time it is rendered down to a small print, the only identifiable feature is the skyline. When coupled with the conventional format, the result is unimpressive. A colleague recently overcame this problem by stitching together a series of images of a seashore cliff to form a single very long narrow image. This was then to be printed a few centimetres high, running continuously along the bottom of the pages, revealing in total several miles of cliff that formed a visual thread throughout the book. This unusual and inventive approach allowed the detail to show and gave a nice control of perspective.

Reproduction size and discernible detail are closely linked. Many an image has been wasted in reproduction because it was reproduced far too small. Detail such as the eggs in this common wasps' nest (*Vespula vulgaris*) are lost in the little reproduction.

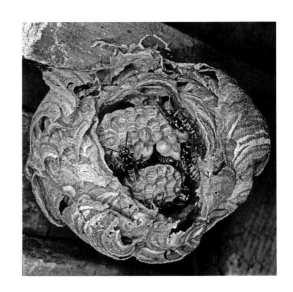

Looking at a wide representation of other photographers' work can provide a whole range of ideas for future projects. The two shots here are from the Wildlife Photographer of the Year Competition 2002. Left: Bald eagles (*Haliaeetus leucocephalus*) against a full Moon, taken at Cape Coral, Florida, USA, was highly commended in the 'From Dusk to Dawn' category. Opposite: A yellow birch tree (*Betula lutea*) contrasting with the forest background at Acadia National Park, Maine, USA, was a winning image in the category 'Composition and Form'.

# Learning from others

Viewing the work of other photographers can provide much needed inspiration, and all photographers should take every opportunity to look at what others are doing. Television wildlife films are made with different objectives and do not have the same intensity of purpose as still photography. To get the greatest appreciation and benefit from the work of other photographers, it needs to be viewed under the best possible conditions. Most book reproductions are far too small to do the originals justice.

One of the world's largest forums for wildlife photography is the annual Wildlife Photographer of the Year Competition, organised by the Natural History Museum and BBC Wildlife Magazine; in 2005, for instance, over 17,000 images were entered. The competition, which has celebrated the work of the best wildlife photographers, both amateur and professional, for over 40 years since 1964, is divided into a series of specialist sub-sections dealing with most aspects of the natural world.

Although the first showing of the best images each year is held at the Natural History Museum in London, the organisers also run travelling exhibitions in many UK and international venues. Each year a book of winning entries is produced so it is possible to scan back through the years and see how the photographic approach has changed. The quality of most of these images is excellent; indeed, it would be difficult to suggest a better reference library of pictures for the aspiring wildlife photographer to study. Looking at lots of high-quality, well-composed images such as these can help to clarify one's personal preferences and form a solid foundation of ideas upon which one's personal style can be developed.

## Wildlife Photographer of the Year 2005 categories

The latest adult categories are:

- Animals in their Environment
- Animal Behaviour – Birds
- Animal Behaviour – Mammals
- Animal Behaviour – All Other Animals

- The Underwater World
- Animal Portraits
- In Praise of Plants
- Urban and Garden Wildlife

- Nature in Black and White
- Composition and Form
- Wild Places
- The World in Our Hands

In addition, there are three special awards:

- Innovation Award
- Eric Hosking Award
- Gerald Durrell Award for Endangered Wildlife

And there are also three junior categories:

- 10 Years and Under
- 11-14 Years
- 15-17 Years

## Self expression and sales potential

The difference between photographing wildlife for oneself and for potential sale can create difficulties with style. Most photographers capture images that appeal to them and if they do so at all, think of sales later. From the point of view of developing a personal style this is certainly the best policy, but from the point of view of maximising potential sales it is much less appropriate. A photographer who has the ability to copy the styles of others or follow an art director's detailed brief has a distinct advantage with regard to sales. It is difficult to switch easily between requirements as a personal style is extremely subtle, very difficult to be aware of and does not normally lend itself to careful consideration – it just happens.

Photographers who create images to express themselves have no such constraints. Style will develop; it is better to worry about consistency in approach and quality. Digital photography makes this immeasurably easier than it ever was in the days of film. It is now possible to produce long series of images with matching colour balance, tonal values and sharpness, even if they were taken in hundreds of different locations and lighting conditions. This is absolutely ideal for the presentation of series of wildlife images that allow comparisons between species and habitats. It also allows a manipulation of images to enhance your own personal style – always provided you recognise your own style in the first place!

## Image collections

Photographic collections are essential tools for many organisations and individuals. The images they contain serve three basic functions: teaching, research and archives; publicity and company branding; and agency collections for sale to publishers or others. An individual collection of natural history images will probably cover aspects of all these uses, making the decisions on how to store and use it all the more complicated.

Teaching, research and archive collections can vary from a few images taken by a single photographer for his or her own use to massive corporate or national collections. For all of them, the essential requirement is that they should be stored in an easily retrievable medium that has good archival qualities. Copyright details should be stored with images but this is often not an issue with older images.

Both publicity photography and company brand images require a photographic style that meets a brief set by a designer or company to reflect the style of a company or organisation concerned. Photographers who can develop styles that meet such briefs can usually give up the day job and turn professional as this is a difficult but valued area.

Many agency image collections specialise in natural history images for sale. The main features they will be looking for are: image quality, impact, clear accurate identification and steady supply. You should expect a continuing circulation of your work if you use them. The human mind has a staggering ability to remember images, almost akin to its ability to remember faces. This creates major problems over reuse. If an image has been widely used it is normally considered as 'dead' and will not have anything like the same impact a second time around. From the photographers' point of view this is a blessing in disguise: it would greatly devalue the impact of their images if the market were to slowly become saturated with an unchanging collection of familiar images for repeated use. The biggest ongoing task in any picture sales agency should be continually presenting good new material to clients and clearing out the old stock. Having vast stocks of images is of little use for sales purposes, since most clients will simply not have the time or patience to plough their way through them. A smaller number of excellent images that are regularly replaced is a much better bet.

From the point of view of photographers who maintain their own image collections sensible precautions to safeguard the copyright and avoid image degradation are necessary. Always code the individual files with your name,

and store the originals separately from the working copy or copies (known in the trade as duplicates, or 'dupes'). If the files are digital, store them on quality CDs or duplicated on a pair of large stand-alone quality hard discs, using a system that can grow as required and will allow access by species name.

The precise length of life of CDs is still somewhat uncertain, but provided they are stored carefully and checked every few years, the risks should not be too high. However, it will certainly be wise to update storage methods as technology changes with time.

A personal style of photography is not solely derived from the technical methods used to create your images, although this aspect is often a major part of it. These pictures of Daubenton's bats (*Myotis daubentonii*) use motion-stopping flash techniques, but also take advantage of the flow of water to evoke the atmosphere of the species' typical habitat, and to make it appear more real than a two-dimensional print.

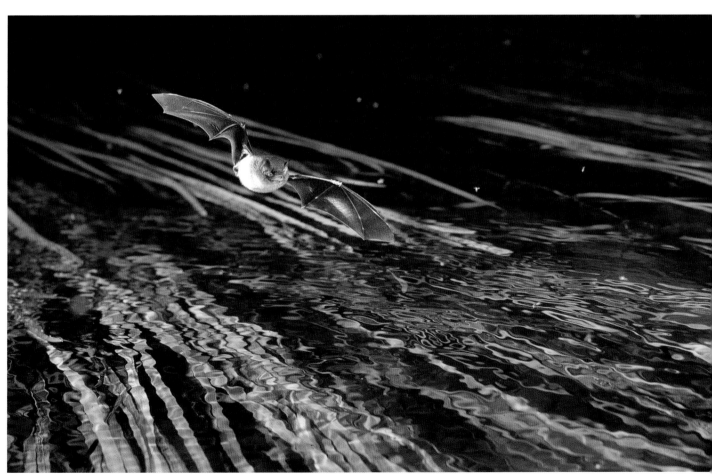

Birds

# Birds

Birds are the most carefully studied and appreciated group in the animal kingdom. Virtually all the Western species have their life histories recorded and lots of species guides, or even detailed monographs are available. Not only have birds been written about, they have long been the preferred subjects of some specialist artists and of early photographers. Try not to be daunted by the wealth of available information: think positive, learn as much as possible, and try and incorporate relevant pieces of information into your efforts; it can only improve the final results.

Over the years, the available equipment has influenced style in bird photography more than any other factor. The history of this subject goes right back to the use of primitive wet gelatine plates during the really early days of photography. Getting close enough to the subject to obtain a decently sized image was the main problem for many years, especially as plate cameras were slow to set up and film speeds were very low.

These drawbacks were perceived by the pioneers of this exciting area of nature photograpy as much as a challenge as a problem, and all sorts of bizarre measures were adopted to achieve the desired goal. Many of these would be considered unethical nowadays. The parental drive of breeding birds to return to their nests and young was exploited extensively to allow the photographer to get close enough. Most of the time, the actual behaviour of the poor bird was not considered at all and as a result pictures of strangely startled or even terrified-looking birds on the edge of their nests were the norm.

The style never really changed until the advent of the 35mm single-lens reflex camera with its big telephoto lenses, although the degree of success of the photographers certainly did. The latter days of the plate cameras produced some superb, almost posed, black-and-white images of birds at the nest. Several photographers were using equipment at the cutting edge of the available technology at the time. Within a few years of the development of electronic flashguns in America, the then massive units were being used for studies on animal movement as well as bird photography in the UK. Much was written in the press about how the flash lights produced a low contrast in the black-and-white images, and even some degree of dislike was expressed by many of the frozen movement in the images.

The advent of truly portable equipment enabled a wider look at birds throughout the year, and nest photography steadily declined so that today it is almost unheard of and mostly frowned upon as unethical. Many of today's bird photographers follow the still growing trend of 'twitching' – rushing off to view the latest discovery of an unusual off-course migrant. Taking advantage of the flexibility of small digital cameras, it is possible to use a small adapter plate and photograph through the telescope that has become an essential item of equipment for every serious bird watcher. Because it is possible to improve the contrast and sharpness of digital images once they are installed on the computer they are quite useable at smaller sizes.

The results of this 'digiscoping', as the technique is known, are frequently available on the internet within hours of the discovery of a rare bird, and are even sent around by mobile phone. Despite the small size of these images, they are often excellent portrayals of the species concerned, especially where the photographer has borne in mind its behavioural features as well as clearly showing the distinctive plumage details to highlight identification.

Taking this a stage further, serious bird photographers carefully select the best aspects of digiscoping and combine them with a slower approach and a wider choice of equipment. They obtain images that put the bird into the context of its habitat and display the aspects of its behaviour unique to its species, while retaining photographic perfection and compositional balance.

**Previous page: Creating opportunities by advance planning is a very successful preparation method for bird photographers. This European goldfinch (Carduelis carduelis) was photographed on a frosty winter morning – large numbers of birds can be concentrated in winter by prolonged feeding close to hides.**

**This page: A beautiful subject approached with good technique and the best of equipment to hand will produce outstanding results, as with these photographs of a white wagtail (Motacilla alba), left, and opposite, of a pied avocet (Recurvirostra avosetta).**

## Getting close enough

Below: A 640mm telephoto lens on a 35mm camera was used for this image of a yellowhammer (*Emberiza citrinella*) bathing in a ford. The car was actually parked in the ford to make the most of light from this angle. The image quality is not brilliant, due partly to the large lens and partly to the 400 ISO film used to make the exposure.

Opposite: Medium-format cameras will produce superbly crisp images but are quite heavy and slow to use or move and as a result images can be somewhat static. This common kingfisher (*Alcedo atthis*) is rather alarmed by the camera's presence, as evidenced by the sleeked-down plumage, ready for flight.

Most birds are relatively small and very frightened of us. They certainly don't like people approaching too close to them. The majority don't like us even watching them with the naked eye, let alone through binoculars or telescopes, as they perceive our gaze as a threat that may mean imminent attack. When you point a new extra large eye at them in the shape of a camera they like it still less and either leave or sleek themselves down ready for a fast escape. With time, they will learn that the danger is not too real and relax. Relax that is, until you press the shutter; hearing the sound this makes, all their worst suspicions are realised, panic overwhelms them and they fly, run or swim away as fast as possible. It can take them a long time to return, often more wary than before.

The quickest way out of these problems is to stay further away, by using bigger telephoto lenses. This is also a good technique to adopt for the photographer with little in the way of uninterrupted protracted blocks of time to spare. However, a major drawback is that big lenses bring with them the technical problems of camera shake and poor image quality. Working in locations where the birds are used to people and thus approach closer is often a better bet. It is possible, for example, to take close-up photographs of normally very wary and unapproachable carrion or hooded crows in zoos, where they habitually raid the feed troughs of the captive animals. It is often a similar story at famous beauty spots where many visitors, intentionally or otherwise, share their lunch with the birds. For instance, the car park at Lands End, Cornwall, is a great site for watching – and photographing – jackdaws at close range, using the car as a hide. There are countless other examples relating to many different bird species.

Looking further afield, all countries have some form of rubbish disposal. These rubbish tips frequently attract large numbers of birds (and other animals) that glean food from among the debris. In the Caribbean, black vultures can gather in thousands at some refuse tips, especially when butchers' offal is on the menu, and they can then be approached closely – although you may have to put up with unpleasant smells. It is a good idea to take your pictures from a car, if possible, as it provides both easy mobility and shade in tropical conditions.

## Specific ideas need specific equipment

Successful photography should not be thought of in terms of luck as to what turns up in the viewfinder; the best images are generally preconceived and require equipment that will fulfil precise objectives.

As well as the potential problems of camera shake and poor image quality associated with telephotos, the perspective created by these lenses may not fit the photographer's pre-conceived idea of what is required in the image. Large lenses produce a very narrow area of focus so while the bird may be satisfyingly large in the frame and beautifully sharp, the surrounding habitat is normally completely unrecognisable. We humans are innately skilled at reading our own species' expressions extremely well, a fact that makes portrait photography a never-ending passion of many people as the depth of information in an image of a subject's face can be outstanding. Unfortunately, we are much less able to read the moods of other species; indeed many animals such as bears and birds are effectively totally inscrutable. Big portraits of these creatures with little other information content than eye contact can quickly become repetitive.

The style of photography that incorporates both habitat and bird necessitates the use of a wide range of different equipment. Standard focal-length lenses, or even wide-angle ones used with small apertures, are the only lenses that will allow both foreground interest and habitat to come into critical focus simultaneously. The remaining difficulty is how to get a camera close enough to the bird while it is behaving naturally.

**Above right:** This image of a white-throated dipper (*Cinclus cinclus*) is a combination exposure by daylight, using a fill-in flash to lighten the shadows. The daylight exposure was necessarily long in order to sufficiently expose the dark streambed surroundings, and so a small amount of movement is noticeable. The fill-in flash part of the exposure has been brief and is responsible for the sharpness of the detail of the insects in the bird's mouth. A long release was used to make the picture, with the camera set on a tripod near the rock and the photographer hidden in the hide (below right). **Left:** In contrast, the picture of the sedge warbler (*Acrocephalus schoenobaenus*) was taken with a telephoto lens using daylight only.

Site selection is very difficult and requires fairly regular visits by the bird, as well as the selection of a background that sums up the features of the species' typical habitat. Such work is normally too invasive to carry out close to nests, but favourite perches are excellent substitutes that should not cause the birds undue disturbance. Camera operating distances may need to be as little as 30-60 cm (1-2 ft) with wide-angle lenses, so actually being behind the camera is normally impossible.

Mechanical or pneumatic camera releases never work well over more than about 6 m (20 ft). This is often sufficient – provided the photographer is hidden in a hide with the camera outside and nearer the bird. Long electric shutter releases offer the advantage of working over greater distances, but entail the transport of drums of cable that may have to be laid over rough terrain. While the cable system will certainly work over moderate distances, setting it up takes a long time and may cause disturbance.

These four images show different techniques using high-speed flashlights as the main or sole source of lighting. Mixing high-speed flash and daylight is always tricky as the exposures tend to be of different duration. A fast exposure for the flash – around 1/1000th of a second or less – and a relatively long one for the daylight – perhaps 1/250th of a second or more. The resulting moving subject will appear as the two images overlaid, one sharp and the other blurred. This is partly visible in the wingtips of the common kestrel (*Falco tinnunculus*), above right. Black backgrounds with flash shots are hard to overcome as is illustrated below left by the picture of the spotted flycatcher (*Muscicapa striata*). The background is too far away to light effectively so as much as possible has been eliminated by the choice of viewpoint. In the case of the white-throated dipper (*Cinclus cinclus*), above left, this is acceptable as the surroundings are so dark. The technique used to take the picture of the northern bullfinch (*Pyrrhula pyrrhula*), below right, is entirely different. Here, a white background has been inserted at some distance behind the bird and lit quite independently from the bird itself. The background is simply a piece of white card set 3 m (10 ft) behind the perfectly wild and free bird in its natural environment.

Furthermore, if the cable length becomes too long, voltage drop can be a problem and require some electronic intervention to cure the fault.

Over long distances or for setting up the system rapidly radio release is, without doubt, the preferred method. Fairly inexpensive model aircraft transmitters and receivers can be modified to release a camera shutter without too many problems, but they often suffer from interference. Again a little electronic tinkering at the receiver end may be necessary so that the camera will fire only with a specific pulse of coded signal. The final method, which is often available ready-made as a camera accessory, is the infrared release. Infrared devices are fine in the studio or outside at night provided the distance involved is not too great and the operation is in line of sight. In daylight, especially sunlight, they can lose their sensitivity. Always test the system extensively before attempting to use it.

Some serious bird photographers even go to the lengths of using miniature CCTV cameras to monitor their still camera viewpoint so they can operate from well out of the bird's sight. The results obtained using such techniques are almost always a one-off for each set-up as birds generally are too smart for repeat performances with very close cameras. Wireless TV systems with a range of 100 m (330 ft) are currently available for about £150.

With a decent radio release system running well it is possible to monitor your bird subject through a telescope from as much as 1 km (0.6 miles) away and eliminate human presence as a disturbance factor. The camera is of course still present and will need some camouflage.

# Using hides

To many bird photographers it is the privilege of being very close to their subjects while themselves remaining unobserved that provides an even greater thrill than seeing the recorded images. Such intimate work involves the use of hides and the sustained input of effort over some weeks. Although nest photography is very dated, there are many other occasions when hides provide the only realistic opportunity for a reasonably close approach. Birds normally need some time to become used to new structures such as hides. Once they are no longer perceived as a threat they will be totally ignored.

When hides are used together with bait or at locations not visited daily by birds, the length of time required to habituate the birds is much lower than at nests or very regularly used sites. Such regularly used situations will need about ten days to two weeks of preparation. You can first lay the folded hide material on the ground and then very slowly unfold and raise it over a period of days. An alternative is to erect the hide some distance away and move it in a little closer each day until a satisfactory working distance is reached. Always keep visits to make such adjustments short – you should aim to be gone within twenty minutes at most but preferably five.

Obviously, at times, such counsels of perfection can be difficult to achieve. An example is provided by the experience of one photographer who constructed a hide in the top of a tall Scots pine in Scotland to photograph grey herons. This tree was about 20 m (60 ft) to the level of the hide and required climbing equipment to reach it. Because of difficulties of access and some problems with wind it actually took three weeks of short visits to finally complete a safe structure. Two different photographic techniques were used to get the pictures from this hide – long telephoto lenses and wide angles set up close to the birds.

When entering a hide, always have a companion to go in with you and then walk away so that the birds think there is

Both these images of common buzzards (*Buteo buteo*), left, and grey herons (*Ardea cinerea*), opposite, were captured on film cameras. A long-release device was used, distancing the camera from the photographer, hidden well out of the way in a distant hide. One of the disadvantages of this method is not being able to see the fine detail of the action at the moment of exposure. A CCTV camera mounted beside the stills camera would have been of great help in circumventing this problem.

no-one left inside. Some birds, especially members of the crow family, can count very well so if you working with such species you will need several people to be seen walking away from the hide.

Be aware that photography from hides can be extremely uncomfortable and you will never work at your best when half numb from lack of circulation. The best plan is to equip your hide with a comfy seat and once in, to stay in for a long session – at least three hours and much longer if necessary.

It is vital to be aware of the fact that the use of hides close to nesting birds constitutes disturbance and may require a licence.

Tidal estuaries and mud-flats can be very productive sites, especially when rising tides press flocks of waders towards you, but a study over a week or two of the birds'

movement patterns will greatly enhance your success rate. As always, there are pitfalls to watch out for – especially the very real danger of your being cut off by a fast rising tide.

If there is any way you can obtain permission to erect a hide it is likely to prove well worth the effort. You will be able to use shorter lenses and have much greater depth of field as a result. Many of the larger birds of prey will come to carrion, such as the carcass of a dead rabbit or a lamb laid out for them. Such shots can often be obtained at long established feeding stations, such as those set up for red kites, but this restricts the scenic possibilities. It is much better and more satisfying to select your own location and persuade the bird to behave as you wish. Be sure to ask the farmer or other landowner if you can work on their land, explain what you are doing and ask them if they can help.

## Interesting alternatives

An attractive alternative to the close approach is a style in which the bird subject or subjects are reduced to a minor but crucial role in what is basically a landscape image. The resulting photographs can be particularly beautiful, with a very natural, relaxed atmosphere, as well as conveying a great deal of the intimate connection between the bird and its habitat. This style is likely to become more popular.

Another interesting possibility is to photograph birds – and other wildlife subjects – in poor weather. This is a relatively untapped seam, perhaps because many photographers are concerned about getting their expensive kit wet. Imagine taking a picture of a peregrine falcon on a rock ledge in driving rain, all greys and blue-greys, with silvery water droplets beading the bird's feathers, or a black and ash-grey hooded crow perched upon a drystone wall in the bleak, lonely expanse of a wet and windy moorland landscape and calling, with head down and tail fanned out.

Whichever style you choose, think out your images carefully before taking them. For inspiration, look at the work of other photographers. It is really useful to be able to see the work of one person over a period of time as opposed to the odd reproductions of those photographers who sell their work. To this end, the internet is a wonderful forum. If you use it regularly and with discrimination, you will find some highly gifted, hugely dedicated photographers from whose work you can learn a great deal.

## Know your bird

As with all natural history photography, knowing what species you are looking at and what is typical behaviour for the bird is fundamental to success. This information will let you know if the bird is shy, or bold and tolerant of people and their cameras, whether it should be in that car park, or if it should actually be on the seashore. All these things can make or break an image.

As well as being aware of such species-specific information, remember that birds are individual characters. If you think about it, it is how they survive. If they all reacted to the same stimulus in the same way 100 per cent of the time, they could all fall prey to the same predator in the same situation. Given enough time, it is possible to get to know birds as individual characters. For us the biggest problem is often recognising an individual in a crowd, but specific behaviour will sometimes allow that recognition. The flight paths of certain individuals are often repetitive, some are bolder than others, some are constantly aggressive, and so on. Particularly with the larger species such character differences can give that little edge that will allow the photographer repeat opportunities on the same photographic theme.

Left: Usually opportunities of capturing interesting aspects of behaviour come only occasionally, and following the action is a necessity. The mating of birds, such as this pair of Eurasian oystercatchers (*Haematopus ostralegus*) is over in a few seconds.

Opposite: Island seabird-breeding colonies – like the one shown here – provide endless opportunities for photography. This can normally be achieved with little or no disturbance to the birds that are actually breeding. Study the colonies quietly from a distance and you will soon find the areas where non-breeding birds gather together. These are usually young birds or those that have lost a mate. It is such groupings that provide continual interaction but will not suffer unduly if slightly disturbed. Choose areas that offer the best lighting and scenic opportunities. These gannets (*Morus bassanus*) were photographed on the Bass Rock, off the Berwick coast in southeast Scotland.

## Opportunistic bird photography

If you are a novice it will pay you to practise on some subjects used to the presence of people. You might even be able to design or redesign your garden with photography in mind. For example, the garden pond or at least a bird bath could be raised up to allow an easy view level with the water surface to make it much easier to photograph birds as they drink or bathe.

If you have no garden, zoos and beauty spot car parks make ideal locations. Try a sunny day in the middle of the week when the place is empty but the local birds have eaten all the weekend sandwiches and are ready for some more. Stay in the car with the window down and watch what goes on for a while. A few crumbs may help start the ball rolling. Decide what you want to do and position the car so that you can see your subject on a level, not looking down at it. A dark cloth against the far window will mask many of your movements but is often not necessary. Never be afraid to move about a bit but be

careful not to move a big lens suddenly. Always move the car to make the best of the light available.

Car parks and other such sites that are often visited by people differ from remoter locations in that the normal rhythms of activity may be disrupted so that birds can make use of the food humans make available to them. Try the same locations at different times of year and even try a fine scatter of seeds applied over several weeks in the winter months. At park lakes, canals, rivers and other water bodies, hot weather brings many bird species to the water and with them a whole new range of photographic possibilities. Easily accessible sites such as these can allow the creation of almost studio conditions with elaborate lighting sets and all the benefits of flash lighting to freeze the action.

Another method that produces good results in the early part of the breeding season is the playback of territorial birdsong. Many songbirds, such as warblers, as well as some other kinds of bird, can be 'called in' very close to the speakers and will often sing in reply to the tape recording. The birds can be quite bold and minimal cover is usually all that is necessary. The chief care that needs to be exercised is that the method is not overused as it may be very disturbing to breeding birds. Do not use it for more than ten minutes in a bird's territory before you move on. Migrant summer visitors when they first arrive in spring are particularly responsive to the playback of their songs. Wood warblers, grasshopper warblers and nightingales respond particularly well but residents, too, such as woodpeckers, will often respond to the correct sounds.

Recordings of the songs and calls of almost all European and North American species are available commercially, but you may have to make your own recordings of species from the more remote areas of the world. Make sure you select an area where you have a comfortable position, the light is good and the approaching bird will have a lot of potential perches that give you a clear line of sight. Play the songs or calls in short bursts and give the bird an opportunity to respond before playing them again.

Left: What will happen next? If you know your species behaviour you will know how long the action will last and what will make the best images, such as this pair of mute swans (*Cygnus olor*) in a courtship display.

Right: Many birds will respond to their calls if played back to them from a recorder. Grey partridges (*Perdix perdix*) will readily respond to recordings of their grating calls from a car hide.

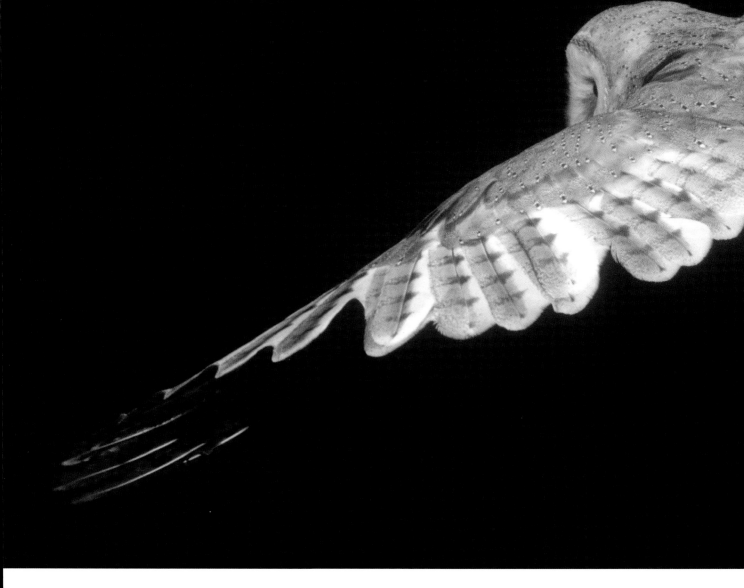

# Flight photography

Modern equipment has made this aspect of bird photography much easier. Long lenses are light in weight and very rapid to focus manually or even use in autofocus mode. Using digital cameras in motor-drive mode allows the rapid capture of a series of images and rapid editing to only keep the best frames. With film, such a multiple-image approach is very expensive, and you have to wait for the results until at least the next day and often weeks later.

Great locations for practising taking pictures of birds in flight are clifftops where seabirds ride the updraughts. Another option is to get a friend or other assistant to throw scraps to gulls on a riverbank or by the sea.

Interaction between animals will always make for good pictures but beware of exactly what you feed if it will feature in your images. Gulls fighting in mid-air over a lump of bread will not look as natural or appealing as if they were fighting over a sprat or other small fish.

Many bird species are declining in the UK for a complex of reasons, including the effects of many modern agricultural practices and habitat destruction. Thankfully the collection of birds' eggs is no longer a major factor. Disturbance is however still a problem. The increasing use of the countryside for recreation means more people are engaged in pursuits that will potentially keep birds away from their

nests or an ever dwindling number of rich feeding grounds. At times this is of little consequence but the potential is always there for serious effects.

The very large flocks of pink-footed geese that have returned to winter on the north Norfolk coast and adjacent farmlands provide a classic example of this. It is estimated that over thirty thousand birds now gather in the area. A careful look at a feeding flock will show that a number of birds always have their heads up and are constantly watchful. These are usually the older individuals with experience of potential threats to the flock. Frequently they will have many years' experience of a particular location at

Opposite, top right and following page: These images of barn owls (*Tyto alba*) were shot in the same location over a period of several weeks. The very different effects were achieved by repositioning cameras. They were photographed by using infrared beam break systems or long releases with the photographer in a distant hide. By contrast, the short-eared owl (*Asio flammeus*), bottom right, was photographed with the camera in the hide with the photographer. It is a good idea to consider and use all the best possible alternative viewpoints or angles of view.

this particular time of year. They may well even recognise individual farm workers and their vehicles and realising they pose no harm, show no reaction. By contrast, you arrive in a different car and behave in a new way and are thus likely to be viewed as a serious threat. For this reason, you should take care to approach carefully and not suddenly erect a tripod or a hide, for instance, or leave conspicuous tracks.

A large flock of wild geese certainly make a wonderful sight as they all rise into the air, but a deliberate disturbance would be totally unjustified. Study the birds and you will learn when they naturally return to the coast to roost, or when the tide causes them to move and where they may go. Then you can be waiting for the geese in an area that will provide great picture opportunities but not stop them feeding.

Mammals

Previous page: All colonial animals, with their continual interactions, make excellent subjects for the photographer, such as these meerkats (*Suricata suricatta*). Becoming accepted by a colony may take quite some time but there is little alternative as the animals can form a very effective interactive warning system.

Left: You will frequently see images of mammals yawning, like this one of a caracal lynx (*Felis caracal*) taken at Tsaobis Leopard Nature Park, Namibia. Contrary to first impressions, this rarely means that they are tired. When stressed, as by the frequent presence of photographers or other people, they often engage in what is called displacement activity. Rather than face up to more stress they do something like yawning or washing. It can actually lead to harm if the animal concerned continually washes the same area or lives at a constant level of stress.

Opposite and following page: Gorilla (*Gorilla gorilla*), opposite left; bonobo (*Pan paniscus*), opposite right; black spider monkey (*Ateles paniscus*), following page top; red howler monkey (*Alouatta seniculus*), bottom. All these primate images were captured from caged animals in zoos. Spending lots of time on these subjects will usually pay dividends. Telephoto lenses are normally the only practical objectives to choose. The backgrounds have been digitally removed. The compounds that were used for photography have either glass walls or raised sections without bars or wire.

# Mammals

The photography of wild mammals is in an altogether more difficult pursuit from all other forms of wildlife photography. The mammals have virtually all learnt to know and fear man. Their senses, especially that of smell, are better than ours, they are relatively intelligent, and most have excellent memories and impressive powers of deduction. This all makes many of them, especially the predators, very difficult to even see, let alone photograph. Apart from approachable individuals in zoos and other animal collections, taking pictures of mammals is not an area of specialisation that can be recommended for the novice or the poorly equipped photographer.

## Using zoos and other animal collections

Photography in animal collections can be a good school for the novice and an alternative location for photographers without large blocks of time to spare in remote corners of the globe. For the professional it is often the only viable financial possibility as no publisher is likely to finance more than a day or two on the other side of the world.

Working with animal collections is different, since you need to use and develop people skills as much as photographic ones. Usually, keepers are very attached to their charges and know their daily activity patterns, often closely related to their own daily routine. In the wild it is the trust of an animal that must be obtained; now you will need the trust of a keeper as well. Five minutes of informed discussion will tell you more than a week's observation. If you explain exactly to the keepers what you want your subject to do, they will first tell you if it is possible with their individual, then (if you are lucky) persuade the animal to do it. It is vital to be well prepared, since your subject may well perform only once, followed by eight hours of total inactivity.

The bars and wire mesh of cages are frequently a visual eyesore in zoos but thankfully most collections have taken steps to eliminate these from vantage points. It is, however, worth mentioning that long lenses and wide apertures are a combination that should throw most backgrounds out of focus. Beware of photographing through thick glass. You will have problems with reflections unless you put the lens hood right up against the surface. It will also give your pictures a distinctly green cast.

Most collections will charge a fee if you want co-operation from the keepers but there is a difference between having a chat and actually asking them to give up some time to help you. A little research will have told you something about the natural and wild habits of your subjects, but each animal is an individual with its own way of coping with captivity. Food and its keeper are frequently the centre points of an animal's life in captivity, so finding out when each are going to appear will mean that you will have an alert and attentive subject for an hour or so beforehand, listening and looking for the first hint of food or keeper arriving. They are likely to totally ignore you but be bright, alert and often well positioned on a high vantage point.

It pays to visit the same zoo regularly rather than lots of different ones. Spending a whole day walking around it will give you time to see various possibilities, and to revisit individual animals later in the day. Drive-through safari parks can pose photographic problems because of vehicle bottlenecks behind you, and the necessity for keeping the vehicle's windows closed. Photographing through curved glass is always a bad idea as it can seriously degrade image quality.

Do heed the warnings about opening windows, however, or at the very least you may lose equipment to monkeys and at the worst your life to a lion. It has happened! Avoid busy days and days with poor light. Snow can be an absolute winner as it hides all the obtrusive backgrounds and lets animals stand out. Make sure, though, that your subject would actually be seen in the wild in snowy conditions. Lions and jaguars are not suitable subjects for snowy settings, but tigers, snow leopards and mountain lions certainly are.

Even in zoos many mammals shun the light and avoid people watching them. If you can get good co-operation from the staff it is sometimes possible to use a remotely operated camera at night to take pictures of smaller, non-dangerous, nocturnal mammals. If so, you could use your car as a retreat and set up the camera in the enclosure, ideally on a well used track or near water or food. You could then watch the activity on an infrared camcorder linked to a screen in the car, and when the animal performs as you want it to, make the actual exposure via a remote release.

Right: Animals in zoos only rarely look relaxed or natural. Also, an unnoticed part of the image can all to easily betray their captive conditions. For instance, in this photo of a sloth bear (*Melursus ursinus*) the animal's bedding is obtrusive.

Below right: It would be a rare sight in the wild to see baby sika deer (*Cervus nippon*) away from dense cover. Zoos rely on their animals being visible to their visitors so dense cover is removed, all too frequently to the detriment of the animals concerned.

Opposite: Like the image of the sika deer fawn this zoo-dwelling sand cat (*Felis margarita*) suffers from an unnatural background. Close cropping, background manipulation or a more careful selection of animal – or zoo – can sometimes help with such problems.

Right and below: These images portraying a white-handed gibbon (*Hylobates lar*) and Siberian tiger (*Panthera tigris altaica*) both have obtrusive chain link fences in the background. Often the shadows cast from these can actually be more visually disturbing than the fences themselves, especially when they fall across the subject. It is sometimes possible to digitally eliminate or reduce these features but it is far preferable to choose a location where the design of the compound requires no fences. Winter snow can often be a photographer's godsend in zoos, hiding concrete, worn ground and tatty backgrounds.

## Gaining trust

While most mammals are very shy, it is possible to build up trust with some individuals over protracted periods. Such relationships can take years to develop, and one false move can destroy months of previous careful work. The great input of time required means that this is not a suitable field for the occasional photographer. Anyone with aspirations in this direction should start by learning their field craft with some common and relatively accessible wild mammals, such as red foxes or badgers, before even thinking of photographing rarities. It is best to leave the photography of potentially dangerous wild mammals to experienced professionals.

Opposite: Many animals have taken to the urban environment and become well used to the presence of people, especially if provided with an incentive in the form of food. These badgers (*Meles meles*) were unconcernedly feeding right up to the open back door of the house on the evening when these pictures were taken. Such situations often allow for repeat performances on following evenings with the opportunity to rectify mistakes.

## Basic guidelines

There are a number of basic guidelines that will be of use to the beginner:

- If you always approach an animal from downwind it will tolerate more noise and movement than if it is made suspicious by your drifting scent as well as the movement. This type of steady quiet approach should also always be made to a fox's earth, a badger's sett or any other mammal's resting place, even in daytime. You can never know when an animal will be awake or even outside sunning itself.
- Approach steadily, avoiding any sudden movements, and don't try to get close.
- Don't stalk the animal if you can see it and don't walk directly towards it. Instead, take an oblique route that will allow you to pass in camera range. Wild animals are much better at being aware of your true intent than most people think. It is best to try and appear to offer no threat whatsoever. If you make eye contact, the animal will almost certainly leave the scene rapidly.
- Clothing should be drab, but it is not necessary to look like a commando. Of more importance than camouflage is soft cloth that has none of the rustling associated with many synthetic waterproofs, instantly acting as an alarm bell to a wary animal.
- Be prepared for very long waits, and pack enough food and drink.

- Most mammals have very structured lives and will be found doing the same things at the same time each day. Use this to your advantage by preparing or entering places to wait for an animal at times of day that you know the animal will be absent. Some photographers even leave old pairs of unwashed socks in such places so that their smell is always present and, hopefully, will eventually cease to be perceived as a threat.

For those lucky enough to know a professional or amateur researcher licensed to fit mammals with radio collars, there may be a unique opportunity to learn the home range of an individual and its resting places, feeding areas and so on. Most mammals are loyal to such sites and a return in the following year should find the animal in the same area, but without an unsightly radio collar. Do not be too misled by the wonderful skills of some cameramen: most documentary films are made using radio-tracking or other hi-tech techniques, or by making use of the knowledge of someone who has been conducting an in-depth study. The camera-work may be excellent and the patience endless, but to ensure they are in the right place at the right time, the wildlife film maker and still photographer alike need someone to share years of work and the necessary technology.

Bait can be very useful as a means to lure animals close to a camera but it has its disadvantages. Animals are often very wary close to bait, and this can show in the images. Opposite: The red fox (*Vulpes vulpes*) in snow has tripped a microswitch when it lifted the rabbit (*Oryctolagus cuniculus*). Right: This image has been made with more care. A fox run passes through this picture and a dead wood mouse was placed just to one side of it. The smell of the mouse was weak but just enough to make the fox pause as it passed. The actual exposure has been made by a passive infrared device sensing the fox's body heat within 15 cm (6 in) of the mouse.

## Recommended equipment

Equipment for either stalking or lying in wait for mammals can be of two types – big telephoto lenses for daylight work and short telephoto to wide-angle lenses for crepuscular (dusk or dawn) and nocturnal flash photography. Both create practical difficulties in use. Because of the shyness, nocturnal habits or love of dense cover of most mammals, your photographic opportunities are likely to be in poor light levels. In consequence the lenses to use must have large apertures so as to gather enough light to make the exposure.

Simply finding your subject through the viewfinder can pose problems when working at these low light levels. Focusing big telephoto lenses when using flash lighting in near-dark ambient conditions is almost impossible manually, and you will need to rely on autofocus if it is essential to use such lenses. It all becomes much easier if you can reduce the focal length of the lens to a small telephoto but still retain the advantage of autofocus. Remember that the little lights on your camera from infrared autofocus, digital display screens or other indicator lights will be highly visible to most mammals, so cover them up in some way that allows you to still read them but prevents the subjects from seeing them.

When you become really expert at field craft it is possible to automate these nocturnal setups with the use of pressure pads, or even passive infrared sensors that detect the subject's body heat. The skill is in knowing exactly what your target animal will be doing at the precise moment when the camera fires. As well as being great fun, this type of photography is widely used in animal research, particularly as an aid to taking a census of very rare animals. However well prepared such 'photographic traps' are, it may take months for an animal of the correct weight to stand on one. The temptation is always to set the trigger threshold on any trap at far too sensitive a level. Then you will be rewarded only by a series of images of leaves blowing past, or a heavy fall of raindrops. At best you may capture a big beetle flying by, a mouse, or other small creature. Photographic traps require a camera that can be fired by the closure of electrical contacts, a feature which is not possible with all models.

To avoid scent problems, flash work normally requires the pre-positioning of most of the equipment many hours or even days before the expected arrival of the subject. Usually the exposure will be a one-off, as the first animal to set off the trap will be frightened off by the flash, so it had better be correct.

The pressure pad is certainly the best method for long-term monitoring of large mammals. Although passive infra-red sensors work at night and in cold conditions, they are a little slow to respond, so fast-moving subjects may be out of frame by the time the camera fires. Micro-switches used together with carefully chosen bait are excellent for long-term surveillance, but can produce poor pictures with just fleeting views of the subject as mammals show great caution when approaching food. Too many have been trapped in the past by bait and caution has become ingrained.

Several different models of break-beam systems are available commercially. This type of apparatus is fairly reliable provided that the system will fire only when two slightly separated beams are broken. This avoids the problems of ultra-sensitivity and the associated unwanted shots of falling leaves and so on, described above. The main problem with break-beam systems is that you need a transmitter and a receiver and the animal must walk between them, doubling the chances that it will detect the trap or the remains of your scent.

Many small mammals hunt by ear for small insects or mice rustling in the dead leaves of a woodland floor. It is possible to mimic these noises electronically to great effect, but always be aware that you may not attract what you hoped to. Owls also hunt using their ears and will be in and gone before you know it.

This yellow-necked mouse, (*Apodemus flavicollis*) took its own picture by breaking a beam. A wild mouse was trained over a period to use one route to a feeding station. Eventually, after it had learned to use one pathway habitually, the pathway could be slowly altered to suit the camera viewpoint.

# Night work

Humans are basically diurnal animals. Our vision at low light levels is poor when compared with nocturnal specialists such as cats, mice and owls. If you include in this assessment the great detail in the 'sound pictures' produced by the echolocation system of bats, we come out by comparison as virtually blind at low levels.

To the photographer this is a major disadvantage, since the camera suddenly becomes a crude tool pointed at a noise or vague movement in the dark rather than a precision instrument for carefully framing and then capturing a specific moment. Fortunately, modern technology has been able to solve some of the problems associated with using a camera in the dark. Autofocus and shutter and aperture data illuminated in a viewfinder are the obvious aids in this connection, although no camera yet invented can on its own become creative and choose the correct moment for shutter release.

For many nature photographers it is the stalking of wildlife subjects to get good photographs that holds the main attraction. However, this ideal is still hard to achieve

Opposite: This badger took its own picture by triggering a photographic system with its body heat. A passive infrared detector sensed its presence on the stream crossing and released the camera and flashlights.

Right: The unexpected can often happen in automated setups. The dead rabbit was laid out by a photographer for a family of stoats (*Mustela erminea*) living nearby. Instead, a common shrew (*Sorex araneus*) looking for beetles on the carrion tripped the passive infrared detector with its body heat.

when working in total darkness. No quality combination of night vision imaging and flash system is currently available that will allow total freedom of movement in the dark. Theoretically it would be possible to design such a system but the market for it would probably be too small for any manufacturer to bother taking up the challenge. The possibilities for the serious researcher into animal behaviour who needs this facility are either, to use the black-and-white rendition of an infrared image captured on the memory stick of a camcorder, or to cobble together their own equipment. As far as the latter alternative is concerned, one option would be to remove the infrared absorbing filter present in front of all digital camera chips and use the small viewing window on the camera back as a night sight as well as a viewfinder. However, this is no easy task and in fact is probably not possible at all on most cameras.

Finding ways of learning what is going on around you in the dark is a technologist's dream and not a viable pursuit for most photographers – with one exception. It is possible to photograph mammals (or other wildlife) in specific

Gardens make excellent test sites for equipment set-ups. The regular path followed by red foxes in this garden was used by an array of domestic pets as well as the local foxes and badgers. All the aspects of the passive infrared system used to create these images could be tested overnight easily, and with no risk to the equipment.

static locations. The method outlined earlier using an infrared camcorder (any model with a 'nightshot' facility) to monitor what is going on, with a conventional camera on a tripod mounted alongside used to make the actual exposures. This can prove very successful, if rather expensive, option. The method can be further refined with some of the new 'micro' models of miniaturised radio TV cameras. The photographer can be about 100 m (300 ft) away, able to watch what is happening on a tiny receiver and release the main camera at the creative moment.

When it comes to animals that move rapidly in the dark, the problems of photography multiply with equal speed. Getting worthwhile images of bats is a classic example of this difficulty. In late dusk it is quite possible to see some species against the sky, but focusing a camera at such low light levels is a matter of luck. Even the fastest autofocus will miss most of the time, usually focusing on the background or infinity. An added problem is that the required illumination has to be on the camera to ensure that it is pointed in the correct direction. This results in the usual problem with camera-mounted flash of flat looking images.

Many bats can fly very fast, some species being capable of attaining speeds of over 60 km/hr (37 mph) on occasion. Besides being difficult to follow with a camera, they are often moving fast enough to require special high-speed flash guns to freeze the movement. Infrared beam-break systems are a must and high power flash very useful for this work. The problems encountered with these animals have encouraged many photographers to abandon trying to get good shots of wild bats they come across outdoors, and to work instead in the studio or with freshly captured animals under controlled conditions in the field. Although this is a pragmatic approach that can produce dramatic images, it can remove the pleasure and challenge from the venture and also will require very specialist licensing in most countries. If it is possible to find a particular spot that your bats will return to with some degree of regularity and work there, you should certainly try this method first.

**Illustrating extremes in the possibilities of attracting animals to bait are these two bats, a soprano pipistrelle (*Pipistrellus pygmaeus*), right, and a lesser horseshoe bat (*Rhinolophus hipposideros*), opposite. These wild, free-flying animals, and have both come to insects offered to them in their normal hunting areas. All the actions required to take these images were automated.**

# Avoiding problems

Suspicion on the part of the subject can destroy many images, but it is possible to reduce it by working in areas, such as popular beauty spots or parks, that are visited regularly by large numbers of people. By always having a background level of human scent that the local animals are used to, suspicion can be much reduced. On the other hand, a distinctly undesirable side effect of this approach can be an increased risk of having your expensive equipment stolen; in certain areas this potential danger can rule it out altogether.

Both rain and condensation can cause great problems with all these automatic techniques. A free flow of air around the equipment is essential, so resist the urge to swaddle your equipment in polythene. It will make the equipment rainproof but soak the contents with condensation. By far the best method is to make your own cover using hard thermoplastic sheets (available from model-making shops), cutting these to the shape of your equipment with scissors.

Allow a space all around the camera by covering it with thick cloth. With a little heat applied from a hair dryer the plastic will then conform to the shape of the equipment. Other rainproof material can be adapted in different ways. Umbrellas can give equally good protection, sheltering while at the same time maintaining a good airflow. They are certainly preferable to big hats or rustling capes when birding in tropical locations during wet seasons. You can buy small umbrellas only 30 cm (1 ft) or so across, and these will double as folding reflectors for flashguns.

When using any of the larger, more complex lighting and camera set-ups, power everything from non-spill jelly lead acid batteries. These are available in a suitable range of low voltages and amp-hours, and will continue to work for days or even weeks in low temperatures and damp conditions. The small batteries used to power virtually all flash guns and cameras are totally insufficient for more than half an hour or

**This stoat is captive in its home cage at a wildlife centre. On its home ground it will behave normally without becoming unnecessarily stressed. When it has had enough it can retire to its den. The problem with taking this picture was mostly the speed of the action. Small animals can move with an almost unbelievable rapidity and seeming randomness which makes them extremely difficult to follow with the camera.**

so of continuous standby operation in good conditions. Give them the job on a freezing cold wet January night and their capability will stretch to only ten minutes or so when you require a minimum of twelve hours.

Check exposures by running a practical test on site. The green leaves of a forest soak up enormous amounts of light and you are at risk of underexposing if you do not test first, no matter what your automatic metering system says. This type of photography takes no prisoners. If you fail, not only have you not got a picture, but you may not get another chance with that animal in that location. Domestic cats and foxes are excellent for such trials although they will quite quickly come to realise that the threat is actually low and avoid the camera trap altogether, so do not overdo the testing. Road casualty animals make excellent bait for red foxes but you may get some peculiar looks from passers by when collecting them!

## Signs of distress

Spotting distress in animals that are being photographed takes a little practice. It can occur in wild animals when the photographer is too close to young or if repeated disturbance is caused in their breeding territory or other sensitive area. With wild mammals distress is usually manifested as repetitive behaviour or constant yawning as though tired, and sometimes there are rapid eye movements. Members of the cat family may stare at you fixedly or become hostile. Bears may suddenly turn very aggressive for no reason at all and should always be treated with respect. Captive animals will start to hyperventilate if stressed and should always be given peace and quiet if they start to pant or breathe rapidly. Once you have become familiar with a particular species, it is possible to spot symptoms of distress very easily in pictures of them.

# Planning a trip abroad

Locations for animal photography abroad abound but to accomplish much on a holiday trip will usually require careful organisation and help from local guides. If your trip is basically a holiday with wildlife interest the best bet is definitely to go for an area with a long list of recorded species, some of which you will be certain to see if your seasonal timing is good. As a bonus, exciting rarities may come your way and it is even possible to increase your chances of seeking some out, but do not be too disappointed if they manage to evade you on a short trip. Examples of such locations are the safari parks of East Africa, the national parks of North America or some of the prime locations in India. All provide good opportunities in excellent light conditions, and guides and vehicles for photographic trips are available.

On the other hand, many people who are seriously interested in wildlife photography generally prefer their own company and want to do things their own way in their own time. Some even prefer to dispense with using guides.

However, even the most experienced travellers occasionally get lost, either by travelling alone or by ignoring the sensible rules set by knowledgeable guides.

Rubbish tips the world over are generally good sites for photographing mammals, even if the smell is overpowering and the background less than ideal from the aesthetic point of view. Many Mediterranean countries have small garbage dumps outside town. These places may be quiet by day, with just the odd dog or feral cat around. By night, however, they may be transformed into major attractions for a whole range of mammals, including such elusive kinds as wolves and civets. Make sure you are aware if bears are a possibility in your chosen location, as bears accustomed to visiting tips are normally very used to people and will not be in the least afraid of you, so posing a serious risk of injury or death. Baited camera traps work well under these conditions, if you can keep the rats from constantly triggering the camera. Even bats can be attracted in numbers to such sites by the flies and other aerial insects also present.

Most rainforest locations are very difficult places in which to photograph mammals (or birds) because of the lack of decent visibility through the dense forest, constant damp conditions or torrential rainfall, and the relative gloom beneath the dense forest canopy. These features make it extremely difficult to obtain more than fleeting glimpses of the larger animals, let alone any pictures other than quick snapshots. On the other hand, this should not put you off if you have never visited a rainforest. It will prove a memorable experience for anyone with a passion for wildlife, and for the photographer it provides the most fantastically diverse array of smaller animal life on the planet, particularly of insects. These smaller creatures alone will make your photographic trip worthwhile and you may still just get lucky with the larger animals. Central America, and in particular Belize, Costa Rica or Panama, have wonderful species lists, good access and forest hotels with guides.

Foreign trips can be full of diverse action on many fronts and it is always wise to have some photographic tasks that will provide record and continuity from such a visit. These bat portraits are selected from a series of pictures taken of all the species collected on one such field trip. The lighting and situations were all standardised in such a way that the actual photography took very little time to set up and take. They show a free-tailed bat (*Ater rufus*), above right; a Peters' woolly false vampire bat (*Chrotopterus auritus*), right; a hairy-legged vampire bat (*Diphylla ecaudata*), left.

Reptiles and amphibians

Because reptiles and amphibians (separate major groups of animals but often collectively known as herpetofauna) are 'cold-blooded' and need to obtain warmth from the sun, both northern and southern temperate regions have a relatively restricted range of species. One has to approach the tropics before the number of species begins to rise quickly.

To the photographer in temperate regions this lack of diversity – and also the shortness of the active season that results from the drop in temperatures over winter – means that careful timing of field trips is essential. Among the amphibians, the great gatherings of frogs and toads that travel across country on their way to spawn in ponds during early spring each year, provide a prime photographic target that allows both a close approach and good light conditions. Similarly with reptiles, the habit of snakes and lizards of warming themselves up on a rock, wall or bank on sunny spring mornings can make for both an easy approach and superb pictures. It is often said that these subjects have been photographed to death but even if this is to an extent true they still make wonderful examples for the novice to practise with. A photographic essay on the life history of the common frog would make an excellent test of both field and studio skills of an aspiring natural history photographer.

Previous page: Some dangerous animals, such as this Cape cobra (*Naja nivea*), can be outright aggressive. Do not believe that your benign intentions will be welcomed or recognised as such or you may become a victim.

Opposite: The identification features of species are frequently their most visually attractive features. In this case the webbed toes and thread-like appendage on the tail tip clearly identify a palmate newt (*Triturus helveticus*).

Right: Locally plentiful species, such as this brightly coloured male lizard (*Calotes calotes*) common in gardens in Sri Lanka, allow repeat photographic opportunities and the possibility to develop approach strategies suitable for each species.

## Important tips for this sort of work are:

- To read up as much as possible in reliable books, magazines and scientific journals on the species you are likely to encounter before you set out.
- To wear rubber boots, but leave a long coat at home or in the car, otherwise as you bend over it will trail in the water. Remember anything you drop is going to get wet so have lots of big pockets available.
- To be aware that often it will be necessary to obtain very low viewpoints. Such angles are almost impossible to view without getting horizontal oneself – which poses problems if you are working in a swamp. It is however sometimes possible to select or create special sites that will allow this. For instance, a ladder laid horizontally between two dry areas may allow you to lie down just above the water surface even over quite deep areas.

- As an alternative, you can build a garden pond with a high retaining wall so that the water level is about 60 cm (2 ft) above the ground, allowing easy water-level viewing.
- If such solutions are not possible, some cameras will allow reflex viewing with the correct eyepiece fitted.

# Studio photography

Many species of amphibians and reptiles are suitable studio subjects as they generally take well to the controlled conditions of captivity. It is possible to purchase from larger or specialist pet suppliers a wide range of species of frogs, toads, newts and salamanders, especially the brightly coloured tropical species, as well as many lizard species and some snakes. These animals may be native to almost any country from all over the world. Always check that they have been bred in captivity and not taken from the wild before buying them and that they appear in good health (a recommendation from someone reliable as to the quality of the pet shop concerned is a good idea, too). Read up carefully on the conditions your subjects require and be sure to keep them at the correct temperature and humidity. Many lizards and several species of snake are also usually available. Buying animals to photograph is a commitment that does not stop with your photography, so bear in mind that this pursuit can lead to extensive collections that need constant care.

The importation or export of protected species is banned in most countries, although many third world states can do little to enforce it. This sort of trade has led to the near elimination in the wild of species as different as various cacti, cockatoos and frogs. Most simply die in transit and those that do make it to point of sale cease to have any conservation value. Effectively they are dead from the moment they are captured. Should you ever suspect illegal trade in animals, always report it to the police.

A frequent problem with animal pictures taken in captivity is a failure to match the habitat and vegetation to the subject's natural habitat. This can be difficult at times but will destroy an image if you get it wrong. It is not usually good enough to take the word of a shop salesperson about where plants come from. Plants are frequently grown commercially in countries far removed from their country of origin and then sold on again, so you will need to identify them and their natural habitat zone yourself – or enlist the help of a knowledgeable botanist. Even woodland mosses have distinct habitats and a temperate forest moss, for instance, would be quite wrong as a backdrop for a poison arrow frog from Central America.

Bear in mind that captive animals can give photographic access to aspects of the life of animals that it may be impossible to record in the wild. Do make the most of this opportunity and go for behaviour and action images rather than static portraits.

The final use of an image is fundamental to its style. Above: The bold outlines from the white background used in this studio shot of the pair of common frogs (*Rana temporaria*) allow this text to be added within the image space and give some freedom to a designer. Left: The image of common frogs taken in the wild is more restricting for the designer but contains more information about how the species behaves.

# Sensible precautions

Handling captive animals is a skill that takes a little while to master. Be sure to wear gloves when touching amphibians as they will resent the feel of your hot, dry skin against their cool, damp one. Some also produce irritating or even intensely poisonous secretions from glands in their skin which you most certainly do not want on your hands. To ensure a natural appearance, watch out for debris sticking to an amphibian's damp skin surface during shoots as it will often do so after handling but is almost never present on free animals. Flash lighting avoids the sharp changes of temperature and humidity that are caused by tungsten floodlighting. Amphibians hate such floodlit conditions but reptiles may well love them until they begin to get too hot.

In the field caution is required with all reptiles and many amphibians you may encounter in the tropics and subtropics, and even with some in cooler regions. Some have a powerful bite, others have toxic mucus, while a very few are both downright aggressive and extremely poisonous. You may be able to get close but this is often only because the animal has seriously effective defence systems and little fear of you. To anyone with aspirations in this field by far the safest option is to apprentice oneself to a sensible and reliable expert, and always do your own homework as well.

Most image collections of reptiles and amphibians are of animals in controlled conditions, captive or at least restricted to a certain extent. It frequently shows in the aggressive poses, over-simplified backgrounds or lack of atmosphere and habitat information in the image. There is certainly scope for a change of photographic style with these spectacular animals to bring some of their wildness into the images.

The problems that will need to be overcome include finding ways to photograph long thin snakes. Snakes are one of the most difficult of subject groups unless one simply concentrates on close-ups of the head. Finding nicely coiled animals is an occasional bit of luck but portraying the hunting animal is altogether another matter.

The experience of a famous snake expert who was trying to do just this with king cobras in India provides a good cautionary tale. These animals grow very large indeed and are exceedingly venomous. He was in thick scrub of about chest height and was sure he was close to his chosen subject, having tracked its trails leading into the thicket. The pattern made by its body in the dust had suggested that it was a large animal and he was, not surprisingly, somewhat nervous. Straightening up to get his bearings,

Tree vipers and rattlesnakes
are seriously dangerous
animals. These images of a
western diamond-backed
rattlesnake (*Crotalus atrox*),
left, and a white-lipped tree
viper (*Trimeresurus albolabris*),
above, were taken with an
expert handler in attendance
and anti-venom on hand in the
studio. Any fieldwork with
such potentially harmful
animals should take the same
precautions.

he was suddenly confronted by an enormous cobra, directly in front and looking down at him. It had already raised the forepart of its body from the coiled section on the ground in a threat posture and was rearing up about 2 m (7 ft) high. Wisely, the photographer backed off, without stopping for a picture.

Recognising when an animal tells you it has had enough of you is part of the skills of any wildlife photographer. It not infrequently happens even with much less imposing creatures than cobras. Sometimes they will simply close their eyes or appear to go catatonic; others may become aggressive. A tight ball is a favourite with small mammals and an icy stare is frequent from the larger predators.

Both these images of feeding amphibians – a common frog, left, and a common toad (*Bufo bufo*) – were taken in studio sets utilising infrared break beam systems. Attention to detail in such situations can make or break an image. The heather in the toad image could have done with another day to straighten itself out a little.

# A golden opportunity

Both reptiles and amphibians are normally shy creatures that prefer to remain hidden, or at least camouflaged. With amphibians all this caution is thrown to the winds for a brief period each year as the animals reproduce.

This extravaganza of activity is seasonal and can be over very quickly in the warmer parts of the world. Usually in the tropics spawning or egg laying starts at the onset of the wet season if there is a regular seasonal downpour. In drier parts of the tropics almost any sudden wet period will do but these are of course unpredictable. In temperate regions spawning is an early springtime event to give the tadpoles time to develop over the summer.

Timing a trip to coincide with the frenzy of activity is extremely difficult without the help of inside information. Using email to contact hotel wildlife guides locally will usually prove the most productive method. One photographer recalls the time when he was lucky enough to be present at

the start of spawning in the rainforest of Belize. The amazing spectacle included many species of tree frog, with several unfamiliar species seemingly appearing out of nowhere. Beautiful red-eyed tree frogs and bizarre Mexican burrowing toads, both of which are rarely easy to see, let alone photograph, were out in vast numbers. The din sounded like a dozen motorbikes being revved up continually.

As usual in such situations it is easy to become distracted from the chief purpose of the trip by the sheer number of opportunities. A good method is to spend some period just looking, identifying and sorting possibilities. Always be aware however that a few species will finish spawning in one night and be hidden again within twenty-four hours. It helps to know which these are beforehand so – to repeat one of the cardinal rules of all nature photography – do your homework first.

Opposite: The low viewpoint in this image of a giant tortoise (*Geochelone gigantea*) on Cousine Island, Seychelles, makes use of the advantages of a wide angle-lens to enhance perspective and depth. Fill-in flash has been used to balance the shadow detail in the tortoise against the backlight from the sky.

Left: Reptiles have the annoying habit of remaining motionless for many hours and then making sudden bursts of movement – not good for a photographer with less than a dedicated amount of patience. Reading up background data or study over a period will show when activity is most likely to occur. With the larger aquatic animals like this alligator (*Alligator mississippiensis*) all the action may happen at night.

Above left: Endless patience is the secret to photographing reptiles, including this Jackson's chameleon (*Chamaeleo jacksoni*). A native of East Africa, it has also been introduced to Hawaii.

Below left: A leopard tortoise (*Geochelone pardalis*) jaywalking along a road in Cape Peninsula National Park, South Africa. Many roads actually pass through our best wildlife areas. Alerting drivers to the danger to both themselves and the local wildlife is a constant challenge to the conservation-minded wildlife photographer. This image could have been improved by retaining the shallow area of focus but selecting a telephoto lens to make the car appear larger and more threatening.

Right: Research into the life cycles of target species is a must for serious nature photographers. There is no other way to ensure that you are capturing natural behaviour. Most animal behaviour is not fixed in a single mode. If it was, it would be a vulnerable aspect of the species' lifestyle that if exploited by predators could lead to its extinction. Normally, within a species, individual behaviour will vary, with a few animals being quite atypical. Turtles normally choose darkness to lay their eggs and for the baby turtles to make their way down to the sea on hatching. This saves many from predators. There are always a few however that will be different, as with these hatchling olive ridley turtles (*Lepidochelys olivacea*) on a coast in Orissa, India. By photographing the odd individual's behaviour, incorrect information is disseminated. Mentioning that it is aberrant behaviour in the picture caption is one way of dealing with this, but it may be better to avoid such potentially confusing situations altogether.

# Insects and other invertebrates

# Insects and other invertebrates

Insects, spiders and the host of other invertebrates, from microscopic water-fleas to giant snails, can be found in every part of the world and every habitat. They provide the natural history photographer with a perfect range of subject matter, with aspects to suit virtually every level of technical prowess. They are immensely diverse, often incredibly numerous, generally not too shy and, for the most part, not so rare that we need worry too much about causing harm by photographing them.

The main problems likely to be encountered are due to the small size of the subjects, and their ability to fly away or hide when disturbed by an incautious approach. Insects are particularly sensitive to changes in the air around them. Temperature, humidity and even concentrations of carbon dioxide can cause them to react. Fast movement will almost certainly cause panic. The visual acuity and colour sensitivity of many species is astounding, but most will ignore a slow-moving, dull coloured object.

## The importance of temperature

There are some species of invertebrate that normally emerge only at certain hours of the day or night but many are active throughout the daylight period, at least giving the photographer a fighting chance of working in good conditions. Insects are 'cold-blooded' and so are not able to regulate their own body temperature; in consequence they become more active as the ambient temperature rises. This is of course within limits, and very hot conditions can cause even sun-loving insects to seek shade until things cool off a bit. This high activity rate, and the associated rapidity of response to stimuli, can pose problems to the photographer trying to creep up on them unnoticed. The sun-basking insect may be gone in a moment: just one noisy or clumsy move is all it takes. In some conditions, the speed of response is so fast that the insect can react to the tiny noise of the shutter starting to release and already be in motion when the exposure is made. On the other hand, the subject will usually soon settle again elsewhere so you can have another try.

Previous page: A seven-spotted ladybird (*Coccinella septempunctata*). Insect communities provide opportunities packed with wildlife interest.

Opposite: It can be tempting to try and add more interest to images of somewhat mundane creatures by artificially introducing either lots of them into a small space or by intimating unnatural behaviour. But it is better by far to concentrate on the subject, its colour form, and the graphic nature of an image, as this photographer has done with this shot of a common garden snail (*Helix aspersa*).

Right: With most insects cool conditions will result in slower reactions. This can be extremely useful when a very close approach is required for particularly small subjects, such as this yellow dungfly (*Scatophaga stercoraria*).

## Getting close to your subjects

Most insects have a sweet tooth, and many like a drop of alcohol as well. A cocktail consisting of a few drops of sweet sherry mixed with some brown sugar and water will hold many subjects in one spot for some time. It is possible to add to the nectar supplies of flowers with a little syringe, and then spend some hours photographing the slightly drunken visitors. Don't worry about giving them hangovers, as insect metabolism is so fast that the alcohol is broken down very rapidly indeed. Insects feed on a vast range of material from carrion to nectar and providing small supplies of it will often hold them close to you for long enough to allow photography. Wasps of several species are great hunters and make fine pictures when cutting up a small piece of meat or struggling with insect prey. Feeding insects is a highly productive photographic technique. It enables efforts to be concentrated into a small area and the repetitive habits of individual insects to be exploited.

Another good method of getting close to your subject depends on the fact that many insects have favourite perches or flowers on which to sun themselves or feed, and will return to them time after time, allowing the photographer to be waiting, already in position. Each of these favourite perches is often used for just a limited period each day, the insect moving on to the next one as the sun moves around. If nothing happens within about half an hour at the one you have selected it is usually worth finding another perch that you have seen used twice within a period of ten minutes or so. Dragonflies, butterflies, solitary wasps, some of the beetles and many of the hoverflies are all excellent subjects for using this approach. Perches receiving direct morning sunlight are especially good for bees, wasps and flies after a chilly night. When the insects are trying to warm up to working temperature, they will bask on the sunny side of a sheltered hedge or fence, where they frequently tolerate a close approach.

If you are using a digital camera, you should make test exposures of the perch and the background to see how the final shot would work out before settling down to await the insect's return. Remember you are in control of making the pictures, and unless you are making images purely as a medium for recording species or other scientific research, you should have some preconceived idea of how the final result will look.

Left: Images of small animals can benefit enormously from being printed large. Detail that is far too small to easily discern directly becomes clear through the magnification. Working out the final magnification of a print such as this earwig (*Forficula auricularia*) is revealing. The insect is approximately 12 mm (1/2 in) long in life.

Opposite: Sand wasps (*Ammophila sabulosa*) are predictable in that they will return to their carefully prepared holes with immobilised prey. This gives the photographer time to prepare. All these images were taken with a Hasselblad camera, an 80mm lens and a modified ringflash. The wasp ignored all the movement and flashes, as it was totally absorbed in its struggle to get the caterpillar into its hole.

Left: Camouflage is always fun to display in images, but occasionally it can be just too effective. The subtleties of colour difference discernable by the human eye are easily lost on film or digital images, and sometimes it is actually necessary to show the animal concerned a little more clearly than appears necessary at the time – as with this crab spider (*Misumena vatia*).

Opposite: Different lighting can alter the entire feel of an image, as shown by this image of a meadow grasshopper, (*Chorthippus parallelus*). Never be afraid to experiment. Digital cameras make this far easier than it ever was with film as results can be assessed at once.

## Background problems

Insects are mostly small, and the main photographic problems revolve around the sharpness of the insect and the background. Because you must focus on the insect itself, the background tends to be a long way out of focus. Matters improve as you reduce or 'stop down' the lens aperture, because the lens simply works better and provides a greater depth of field to the image. Some single-lens reflex cameras allow you to view the image with the lens stopped down, but it will appear very dark because the small aperture lets very little light through the lens. Using a digital camera, it is much easier to see the image on the little camera screen.

To complicate matters further, the focal length of the lens that you are using will profoundly affect the apparent amount of depth of field that you can obtain in any given situation. Telephoto lenses, with their long focal lengths, will give less apparent depth of field than wide-angle ones, which have short focal lengths. The effect is proportional. Many macro lenses ostensibly designed for close-up work are in fact macro telephoto lenses and suffer from the apparent lack of depth of field common to all telephotos. The benefit that they do bring is the ability to shoot from a distance and not disturb the subject too much. Wide-angle macro lenses will give the greatly increased apparent depth but necessitate a close approach.

The choice between the two must lie with the requirement of the individual photographer. When the insect subject itself is of prime importance, as in a picture taken for identification purposes, then the macro telephoto lens is the one to use as its speed of use will provide adequate pictures of most subjects with minimum fuss, while dropping backgrounds completely out of focus. If the habitat, surroundings and final impact mean as much as the insect itself, then go for the wide-angle macro lens – but remember that you will have to put up with the frustration of significant failures from the disturbance of a close approach.

# Invertebrate identification

The identification of insects and other invertebrates can be a little daunting for anyone with little or no experience of such matters. The sheer numbers of species involved is staggering, even in the temperate regions of the world. Many only have scientific names and if you are in remote regions then some may not even yet have been given these. Species from any of the more obscure groups will require a good deal of ancillary data to allow any hope of identification from the photograph. Features such as location, date, food plant and behaviour all need to be carefully recorded.

If you turn up at a museum with a collection of photographs for identification you should expect to be charged for the service. In many instances the insect itself will still be required to enable positive identification. The collection of insects is still regarded as normal practise by professional entomologists; however, do not expect it to be viewed this way by conservationists, it may even be a considerable legal offence to collect or export them, alive or dead. Professional entomologists have collection permits as a matter of routine and do expect that anyone interested in insects will have the same legal papers.

All this can and does lead to identification problems but it should not mean that you should give up trying. Offering collections of images to museums by way of payment will occasionally bring forth identifications. All too frequently there is no link between the habitat or behaviour of an animal and the dead faded museum specimens in a drawer. Colours usually become paler or duller in older specimens and your images may well be of considerable use for descriptive texts. The example that follows is one of several that demonstrate this value of photography to zoology.

High in the forest canopy of Belize lives a large kingfisher-blue cricket. In the same forests one often hears a sound remarkably like a very loud dentist's drill. A visiting photographer collected several of the bright blue crickets at a small portable ultraviolet light trap. Fascinated by these exotic insects' colour and immensely long antennae, he

made several pictures of them before returning to the UK. Thinking that so large and obvious an animal would be easy to identify, he had not returned with any specimens.

A look at the appropriate reference books soon made it obvious that his task was not going to be so easy. Among the dozens of crickets from Belize were none that resembled his photographed specimens. Not wishing to give up, he visited the Natural History Museum's Department of Entomology and asked to have his photographed specimens identified. Eventually this was achieved but the difficulty was that no one had realised that the species was electric blue or indeed that they were nocturnal and attracted to UV light. The only specimens in the collections were a pale buff colour, having faded over time, but were without doubt the correct species. The photographer's interest in this particular species had led to his work providing scientists with another piece in the jigsaw of knowledge about the Belize rainforests. The information he received in return, besides a scientific name, was an answer to the puzzle of what produced the imitation of the dentist's drill. It was his electric blue cricket.

**Fresh from the treetops, these lively blue crickets (*Moncheca pretiosa* Walker) were not identified until it was realised that the Museum specimens in collections had lost all their colour.**

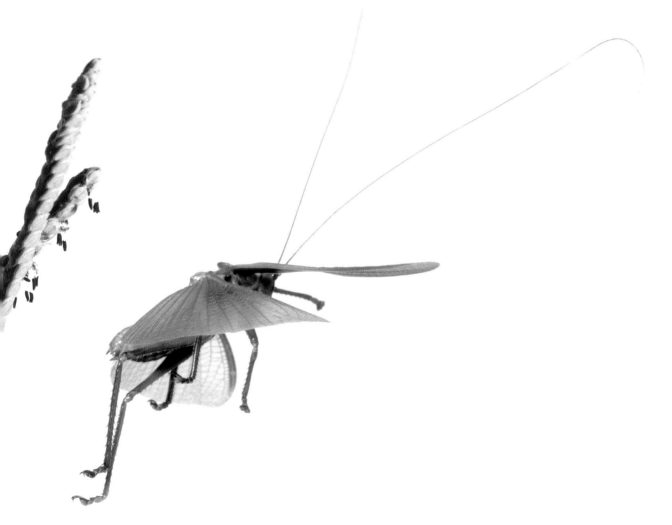

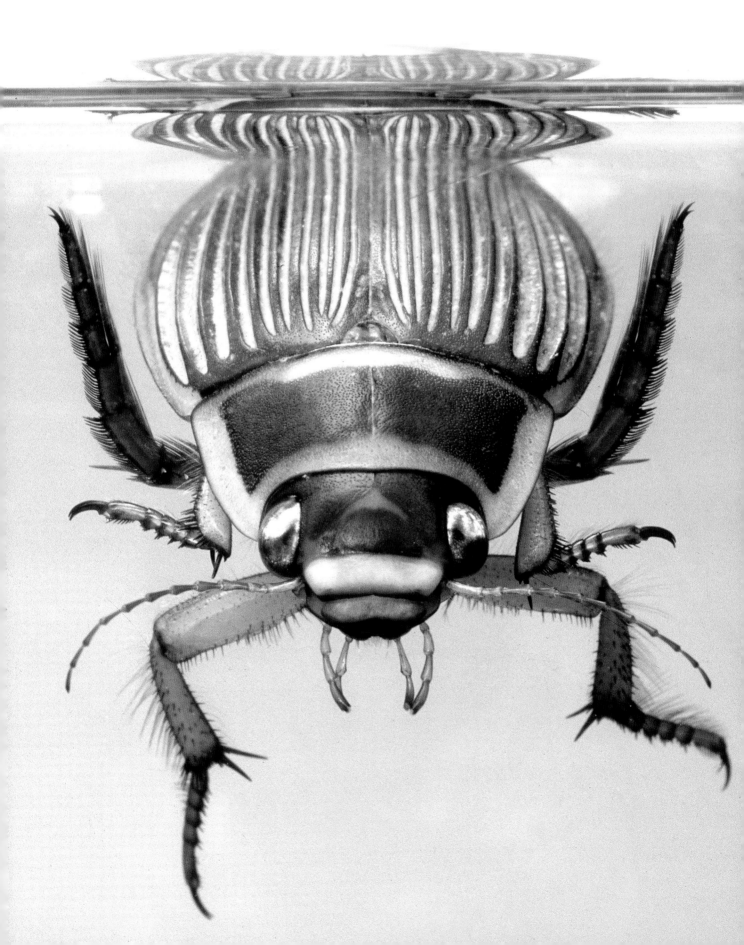

Opposite: To take this image of a great diving beetle (*Dytiscus marginalis*) a tiny, thin-walled glass tank was used to hold the beetle briefly. Working close to a pond allows fresh, active animals to be photographed and then quickly returned to their environment.

Right: Anything that will cause an active insect to pause its constant movement is of use to the photographer. Studying the life histories of insects can help. This male scorpion fly (*Panorpa communis*) sucks insect juices as food but will also offer them to prospective mates. While eating or waiting it is normally quite oblivious to the photographer's presence.

## Tips from the specialists

Many photographers who work with insects have developed all sorts of tricks to allow a close approach and to slow down their subjects' reaction time – though, regrettably, not all of them are ethical. Some specialist photographers work in the studio under controlled lighting conditions, rear their insects through to maturity to produce immaculate adults, then keep them briefly in the fridge to slow them down before photographing them.

Working in the studio certainly has many advantages for the use of complicated, high-speed setups using flash coupled with beam-breaking systems. The studio is a dry, safe, controllable environment where you can repeat attempts easily. But here, as in the field, your ability to predict how an insect will react to stimuli is as important as your skill with the equipment itself.

In such situations it is worth noting that individual insects of a particular species can have different temperaments and if one will not co-operate, it is certainly worth persisting with several others. Often, working with insects straight from the garden is a good plan; they behave obligingly for a few minutes and can then be released straight back out again

after you have taken your pictures with a total time in captivity of just ten minutes or so. Insects left in captivity for any length of time are loath to do anything at all, and – not surprisingly – often behave as if they are in a bad mood. Individual workers from groups of colonial insects, such as social bees, wasps and ants, resent isolation and will quickly die in captivity. An hour or so is about the most one can expect of them before release is necessary. It is sometimes possible to capture insects in the act of seizing or dealing with prey; they are usually obsessed with this and will continue with the activity while you quickly transfer them to the studio and grab some quick shots before an equally rapid release.

Photographing behavioural responses in captive insects is much easier than with any other animal group. Most insects have to go to endless trouble to meet up with other members of their own species, especially individuals of the opposite sex. Some insects and many spiders run a grave risk of being eaten by their prospective mate when they finally do meet up, so the actual meeting can often be a careful business.

To avoid missed feeding or mating opportunities, evolution has made reaction to these encounters essentially instinctive. The surroundings and close events are normally ignored. With a little care, introductions can be arranged under controlled studio conditions, or even in the field, with every prospect of a significant response.

One species of strikingly coloured black and yellow solitary wasp preys upon vine weevils. The wasps will sit happily in dark conditions on flower heads in the studio for quite some while. When presented with a vine weevil and brighter light, they suddenly spring into action and will sting the weevil several times to paralyse it, then carefully load the proportionately huge weight underneath themselves and fly off out of a deliberately left open, studio door. As soon as

the action starts, they are totally oblivious to all lights, flashes and cameras. The weevil is all that matters. Obtaining prey certainly ranks higher in the survival stakes than the fear of a few cameras and lights. This is also worth remembering if you are ever tempted to film big cats from unprotected locations!

As with various other groups of animals, insects use sound extensively for communication and territorial defence. Crickets and grasshoppers are among the best-known examples. With many grasshopper species it is the males that call extensively, and on a sunny afternoon they will attract each other until a group is formed, all calling in competition. By using pre-recorded calls on an endless tape loop it is possible to bring many species down out of

Opposite: While this photograph of a brown hairstreak butterfly (*Thecla betulae*) makes the subject perfectly clear and a wonderful exercise in the representation of subtle colours, this insect is actually incredibly well camouflaged. It is on the wing in very late summer when many dead leaves are around and is almost impossible to spot on a drought-affected twig.

Right: Colour in a subject can be overpowering. Many digital cameras have a very high internal default setting for colour saturation. With subject matter such as this moth/plant combination it is often advisable to control it. The moth is a fairy moth (*Adela reaumurella*).

the bushes or in from the surrounding area, close enough to allow photography. Select the site carefully and make sure that your target species is already calling in the vicinity. Then sit down quietly and await developments. This trick can take a while to work so do not try and rush things along as soon as you spot the first insect approaching. Very slow movements on your part are essential to success.

Just what can be achieved by careful lab photography was beautifully illustrated over forty years ago by a groundbreaking television film on the life history of a species of wood-boring wasp, its parasite, and the hyperparasite that lives on the parasite. This film was the first to attempt such detailed and magnified recording of natural behaviour in insects under controlled conditions. The fact that it was

possible to obtain and record highly complex natural instinctive behaviour even under the conditions then required to film, conditions far removed from an English woodland, inspired many further works and formed an important early milestone in the development of the long tradition of fine natural history films on British television.

Many of the more successful professional photographers specialising in taking pictures of insects have developed field techniques that allow a sure speed of response to a situation together with the production of high-quality images and a very high success rate in achieving exactly what they want to see in the final result. This approach is necessary in order to obtain the regular flow of images required to provide an income – a far from easy task.

## Planning ahead

The individual who needs the images for their own use may not have large blocks of time available and must develop an effort, perhaps sustained over years, to coincide with the seasonal activity of the adults. For most types of insect this period is extremely short – in some cases it is only a few hours for each adult generation each year. Planning as far as a year ahead may be necessary in order to be in the right place at the right time. As always, the end use of the images must be kept in mind, and the input effort matched to the requirement.

Insects are found across the world, almost – but not quite – from pole to pole. In Arctic regions insect activity is brief around midsummer, with the rest of the year spent largely inactive. Some insects there gather in immense numbers; the best known (and most notorious) examples are the swarms of biting mosquitoes and blackflies. Arctic insects can be found over land where snowfall is sparse and the tundra is exposed in summer. It is these huge clouds of insects that attract so many bird species to breed during the brief summer in the Arctic regions – and repel so many human visitors! Although individually they are not the most inspiring of photographic subjects, when massed together in swarms these insects can become that special ingredient of a picture that gives it authenticity and life.

Moving from these cold regions where insect variety is low into the temperate, subtropical and tropical regions, the diversity and size range of insects increases. However, it is only close to the tropics that the really large insects occur. Of the tropical habitats, the most productive by far are the rainforests. For anyone interested in photographing spectacular insects of a huge variety of species a visit – or visits – to a rainforest is a must. A tiny light trap can attract hundreds of moths, beetles, flies, wasps and hornets of a great number of species every hour. Many of the moths rival bats for size and the largest beetles approach the size of cricket balls. As always care is necessary when handling insects like this. They can have quite unexpected defence mechanisms, such as sharp spines or irritant hairs. The strength of the large beetles is amazing. Hornets are frequently caught in light traps, so take extra care when emptying them. Most large crickets have very powerful bites and several are fiercely predatory so gloves are a good idea for these species.

Rainforest weather is often at its finest in the morning with rain falling in the afternoon, before clearing overnight. Try to make photographic walks early on in the day before it gets very hot. Use flash or have a helper hold a silvered reflector

Opposite: Defensive hairs on animals need to be treated with great caution. Some tropical species actually have hypodermic hairs containing powerful anticoagulants. Never touch hairy caterpillars, such as this great peacock moth larva (*Saturnia pyri*) with your bare skin unless you are certain of its species and know it to be harmless.

Below: Large groups of insects, such as these monarch butterflies (*Danaus plexippus*) or for that matter any other animals, pose particular photographic problems. These include retaining the individual identification while still showing the mass, coping with the very large depth of field required, and not disturbing the subjects.

to illuminate shadows as the tropical sun will otherwise make them appear very dark indeed. Always have a pocket full of collection boxes ready to move some of your subjects to more suitable locations for photography or take back to your lodgings or camp for better identification before release. Never touch hairy or spiky caterpillars directly with your skin as many will cause severe allergic reactions.

With great care and very slow movements it is possible to approach some of the nests of colonial wasp and hornet species, but this should be done only when you know exactly what groups you are dealing with. The infamous killer bees of the Americas (hybrids resulting from an accidental release in 1957 of an especially aggressive subspecies of African honeybee during a scientific experiment in Brazil) are not just miniature monsters of the disaster-movie producer's imagination. Able to travel 60 km (37 miles) on a single meal of honey, they have over the years steadily moved north at an average of about 400 km (250 miles) a year, reaching Mexico in the 1980s and Texas and California in the 1990s. Their much greater aggressiveness compared with the native hive bees and their habit of swarming much more often means that they can inflict far more stings on people in a shorter time. They can cause terrible pain and even death. So it is probably best to avoid the nests of any insects resembling wild honey bees in Central or South America.

The wood wasp (*Urocerus gigas*), opposite, is not actually a wasp at all but a sawfly – a better name is horntail, which refers to the prominent ovipositor (egg-laying apparatus) protruding from the end of the body. It is a major pest of softwood timber as its larval stage is spent eating the wood as it tunnels through tree stems. This insect is a host for the parasitic ichneumon *Rhyssa persuasoria* (below left) – one of the true wasps – shown here in pupal stage. The ichneumon wasp uses its long ovipositor to lay eggs on the wood wasp grubs deep in the wood. Then, in turn, *Rhyssa* is attacked by another ichneumon parasite, *Pseudorhyssa* (above left), which lays its eggs in the *Rhyssa* grubs in the same way. This wonderfully complex story makes an ideal subject for photographic illustration.

Water

Serious underwater field photography is a highly specialised area and really requires a complete book on its own. There are, however, many aspects of this field that can be tackled by many general nature photographers, provided that they have some studio space and a little in the way of DIY skills. Much freshwater life can be kept in aquariums with little fuss. Anyone contemplating this rather exclusive branch of photography should start by gaining as much advice as possible from books, magazines, specialist aquarium suppliers and, if possible, experts on the subject, about keeping and maintaining a home aquarium.

There are many pitfalls that need to be overcome regarding the initial establishment of tanks for housing your subjects. Despite this, there are some straightforward tips that are worth taking into account:

- Aquatic insects and small fish, or even water plants, need to settle down and acclimatise to their new conditions before they will look and behave correctly. Stressed individuals look (and probably feel) terrible.
- Saltwater aquaria are considerably more exacting to establish and maintain and are likely to prove expensive unless you are very close to the ocean.

- Within reason, the bigger the better is a good rule of thumb when thinking of a holding tank.
- After the initial setting-up and settling-in periods these holding tanks will function for many years with very little maintenance. The individual water quality requirements, (particularly the pH or specific gravity of the water in a saltwater aquarium) can be quite specific for fish and it would be very wise to investigate the specific requirements of any intended groups when you set up your holding tanks.
- No animals can be added to the tanks until bacteria become established that will remove the waste products that the fish or other animals will produce. This can take about six weeks but depends a lot on the tank temperature and what is present in the water when the tank is set up.
- Initially, keep the stock levels very low and raise them only slowly. This allows the bacteria that control the waste products to keep in balance with the production of waste. If you do not follow this procedure, you will certainly have a very smelly tank and a lot of dead animals.

Previous page: A spotted eagle ray (*Aetabatus narinari*) in the Galapagos. For most of us such photographic opportunites are rare and all too brief. The temptation to grab the camera and shoot away can be strong. It is better to acclimatise and get to know the animals and topography before picking up the camera with a better purpose.

Left: The water purity requirements of crustaceans, such as these signal crayfish (*Pacifastacus leniuscus*) are even more demanding than for most fish. High circulation rates, good filtration, very low ammonia levels and carefully controlled pH are all usually essential to maintain a healthy tank for these invertebrates.

Opposite: Huge display tanks with complete underwater environments are open to the public in many major cities. The blacktip reef shark (*Carcharhinus amblyrhynchos*) shown here was photographed in such a tank. Pitfalls to beware of are reflections, scratched glass and the green cast produced in images by the thick glass of the tank walls.

## Specific problems

Photographing objects under water in tanks follows basically the same rules as conventional studio photography, but there are some specific problems. The major problems are due to reflections bouncing off the glass, scratches on the glass or coloured water. Backgrounds in tanks tend to be dark and it is worth paying some thought to this when the studio tank is set up. Keeping freshwater or saltwater plants in tanks as backgrounds is difficult and will require special bright lights rich in ultraviolet light to keep them growing; this is especially true for marine algae. Water animals, some fish excepted, have a habit of remaining immobile for very extended periods of time and then suddenly bursting into action. To undertake action photography under these circumstances is not for those lacking in either patience or fast reactions. Indeed, much still remains to be accomplished in this field of underwater action. Just one example that remains to be photographed are images of a dragonfly nymph actually in the act of extending its mask to capture its prey. There are plenty of film sequences of this fascinating behaviour, and photographs showing the nymphs eating, but no stills are known showing the actual moment of capture.

Right and opposite: Working close to a pond overcomes many of the problems of keeping specimens for extended periods. Reflections can be a problem, but may be dealt with by the use of lots of black cloth around the camera. A 'V' section tank will further reduce reflection as well as keeping the subject matter off the tank bottom.

## Isolation tanks

To compensate for the immobility of many subjects, the colour and shape of many aquatic crustaceans, insects and other invertebrates can be spectacular. There are several ways of capturing good images of these creatures and overcoming the problems of dark dirty backgrounds of tanks that can be so distracting. By creating a tank within a tank it is possible to isolate the animal and at the same time restrict its movement to a particular plane. The little interior tank can be constructed from quite thin glass and bonded together with silicone rubber. Care needs to be taken to avoid scratches or smears of silicone but otherwise construction is quite simple. The separate little glass panels can be supported with sticky tape until the silicon has cured. It is a good idea to leave the mini-tank for a few days to allow the

smell from the silicone to dissipate before use. The size and shape of these little tanks can be adjusted especially for each job. One of the most useful is a 'V' section tank that keeps animals off the bottom of the tank. If a plain white, or coloured background is required, the little tanks can be used on their own filled with clean, carefully filtered water from the holding tank. Do not use water from other sources as it may have very different properties and upset your specimens. Nothing looks as unhappy as a sick fish. Filtered water is essential as any tiny animals or particles will catch the light and be awfully intrusive in the final images. Many aquatic animals shun light and will react very badly to continuous bright light. Flash works well, however, provided you have just enough light to focus.

## Dealing with lighting

Lighting for these little glass constructions is difficult as the light can bounce between the flat glass sides and eventually come back into the lens to create reflections, bright spots or highlight scratches on the glass surface. For this reason it is useful to use flash that has built-in modelling lights. Using this it is possible to see all the reflections and make the necessary corrections before exposing, something impossible to do without the modelling lights. You will, though, need to allow some time for the tank inhabitants to calm down again after checking for reflections with the modelling lights.

It is a physical property of light to disperse as it hits water. This has the powerful effect of lowering the contrast of the lighting on objects under the water. Flat-looking results have been rather the norm with pictures taken in tanks; thankfully it is now possible to lessen the problem with digital images by careful after-treatment using computer software.

# Acclimatisation

As with the photography of terrestrial insects, fresh aquatic insect specimens normally react better to the artificial conditions of a tank than ones that have been in captivity for some days. It is better still if you have a garden pond from which resident animals can be borrowed for half an hour or so. Make sure you are careful to match the temperature between your photography tank and the pond.

Fish and crustaceans often have specific fresh and marine habitats to which they are physically suited. Many of these species like a flow of water to swim against or hide from. Specialist tanks can even be created to mimic the highly aerated conditions below small waterfalls or the action of little wave surges against coral. Rather more care is required in construction than with making the little interior tanks, and thicker float or plate glass is required for the walls, but the rubber will hold it together and keep it waterproof. The creation of high water-flow conditions can be a major challenge requiring large pumps, but will produce beautiful images in ways almost impossible to capture in the wild.

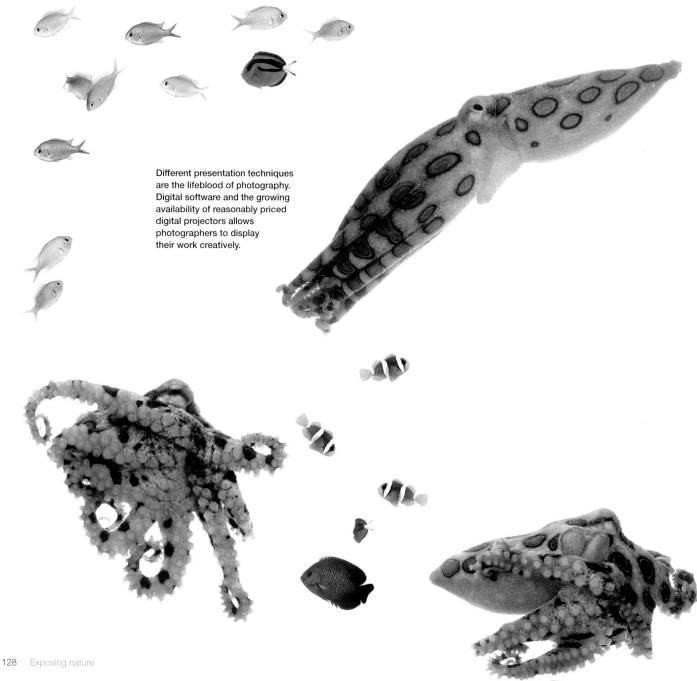

**Different presentation techniques are the lifeblood of photography. Digital software and the growing availability of reasonably priced digital projectors allows photographers to display their work creatively.**

# Coping with reflections

Reflection of the sky from the surface layer of water is the chief cause of our inability to see clearly into the water below. As light is reflected, it becomes polarised (that is, its electromagnetic vibrations are restricted to a single plane, in contrast to ordinary, unpolarised light, in which the vibrations are in all planes perpendicular to the direction in which the light waves are travelling).

Provided that the surface is unruffled by a breeze or ripples much of this reflection can be eliminated by the use of a polarising filter. The filter must be rotated until the best effect is achieved. Unfortunately the filter itself is quite dark and requires an exposure increase of about one stop of aperture. The effect of this type of filter is to allow a much clearer picture into the water below. At the correct angle the elimination of reflections can be almost total. The worlds beneath the surface of clear, smooth rivers or seashore rock-pools become possibilities as photographic subjects, together with the abundance of life that they contain.

Even with the use of a polarising filter subject distortion still remains a problem. Distortion is caused when you look obliquely into water. The light forming the image is bent, stretching and flattening the image of what lies below the surface. To minimise this, try and keep your camera angle as vertical as possible, with the plane of the film or digital chip nearly parallel to the water surface.

**Right:** Reflections are not always problems and can be used creatively to concentrate interest on a specific area of an image, as with this one of a European grass snake (*Natrix natrix*).

## Underwater photography

Even using all these techniques, photographing through a water surface is less than ideal. You can buy elastic waterproof jackets for cameras, that will allow the camera to be immersed to a depth of a meter or so without the need to resort to a proper waterproof camera housing made especially for your model. If used only a few centimetres below the surface, these plastic housings allow control of the shutter without too many problems. Go any deeper, and the plastic is pressed close against the body of the camera,

making it very difficult to operate. The benefits of lowering your camera into the water – avoiding reflection or distortion – will be immediately apparent in the results. An alternative method for simple underwater photography is the waterproof disposable camera. Beware, though, of problems with focusing as some of these cameras have little in the way of focus setting. All these underwater techniques are very much 'point-and-press', unless you want to put your head under as well to look in the viewfinder. Here the

Left: Dive photography requires all the skills of the photographer as well as the expertise of a diver. It is certainly demanding, expensive and time consuming, as well as extremely rewarding when the results are as good as this picture of a shoal of blue and gold fusiliers (*Caesio teres*) taken off Sipadan, on the island of Borneo.

Below: Seashore rock pools are treasure troves of wildlife and colour. Recording them takes care, and a great deal of time to identify exactly what you are looking at. Beware of tinkering with what you actually see to 'improve the image'. In this case the razor shell (*Ensis*) is out of keeping with the rest of the image as it is a species of deep sand beaches.

small simple digital camera will score every time, as you can check your results at the site and re-shoot as necessary.

Although underwater images can often be flat and lacking in saturated colour, a well chosen habitat such as a rock-pool and an understanding of what is involved will give you every chance to portray a stunning array of saturated colour in crystal-clear water. A rocky seashore on a quiet summer afternoon can make a very pleasant and productive studio until the tide returns.

Plants

# Plants

If the identification of insects often poses problems, the identification of many plant species can be even more difficult. To become even mildly competent in one general area is a considerable undertaking. To thoroughly understand the requirements of individual species and display them within an image requires a fair amount of background research as well as searching for the ideal example that fits the photogenic prescription. Most plant photographers have a set of such species' prescriptions lodged in their heads for each season. Every time they go out, they search their surroundings for specimens that illustrate to perfection the entire plant, its flowers, its location, the soil type, the degree of exposure, the surrounding scenery and maybe other features such as leaves or fruits – not to mention that indefinable something that makes a picture special.

More than any other branch of natural history photography, plant photography gives rise to large personal collections of images. The different appearance of each plant through the seasons and the large numbers of closely related species means that comparative collections can be particularly valuable, even if just for personal reference purposes.

Making the images in these collections accurately comparable can prove a real difficulty with this sort of photographic work. Long gaps in time between photographic sessions means that inevitably the natural light will be at

different levels, directions and colour temperatures from previous sessions. Imagine the difference between early spring sunlight on a woodland floor and the way it will look in midsummer. It will change from a relatively harsh, blue light from the open sky to dappled green light filtered through the canopy of leaves – quite a range to cope with. Furthermore, if you use film, you are almost certain to have a different batch in the camera if not even a different make, which may produce a distinctly different colour balance. Even changing lenses can cause a noticeable alteration in this respect. All these separate changes from the previous session mean that the new images will look very different from the first set and be rather less than comparable.

Previous page: This Australian coral tree set in the monoculture of a Sri Lankan tea plantation may not be a very natural landscape but certainly makes a colourful saturated image.

Below: From left to right these images of a downy birch tree (*Betula pubescens*) effectively capture the transition of the seasons, from spring through to winter. They also highlight the principal advantage of landscape photography – the possibility of returning to the same subject at different times of the year, and for many years to come.

Illustrations of single flowers can frequently lose the feeling of the natural habit of a species. In early spring, wood anemones (*Anemone nemorosa*) form living carpets of delicate white flowers in open deciduous woodlands. The problems involved with showing a small plant in detail but at the same time having a feel for the woodland habitat can be extreme. Here, wide-angle lenses have produced the required depth (left and below). When using these wide lenses, take care not to include your shadow, avoid camera shake with the slow shutter speeds at very small apertures, and pay constant attention to the angle of the horizon (opposite top). Also be aware that in such a picture as this it is very easy to overexpose the bright white highlights (opposite bottom).

In a similar way to the wood anemones on the previous pages, these pictures of lesser celandines (*Ranunculus ficaria*) have been designed in different ways to set off the image styles to best advantage. The image creation process continues long after the moment of exposure and is often aided by a designer's presentation skills. Timing is the key to showing plants at their best. Arriving to photograph on exactly the right day (and even the right time of day) can make the difference between average images and show stoppers. The plants in these three images are the same, but with a gap of ten days between images. The two main images were illuminated by daylight and then digitally colour matched using a greyscale, as shown in the smaller image. Such greyscales are excellent for this purpose but much less so at matching contrast. The white patch in the greyscale is a matt reflected white, while the highlights in the images are actually spectrally reflected (mirror reflected) sunlight with a very high ultraviolet content. These bright highlights will always be brighter than the white of a greyscale. It is best to adjust the contrast by eye and the colour by the greyscale.

## Obtaining consistent results

Even differences between using digital and film cameras can make any natural lighting used likely to be quite different in effect. The answer to these problems is to use a system that allows the lighting conditions used to make the exposures to be replicated exactly time and again. Basically this is a sort of mobile translucent tent that is put over the subject and illuminated from above by flash. Care still needs to be taken to use the same camera and flash on each occasion. These little plastic tents are commercially available in a range of sizes and will pack up into an easily transportable bag without too much trouble. If you use film you will still have some problems with film and processing consistency, but for the most part the images will be greatly improved. If a greyscale or small piece of grey card is included in an image at each session it will allow an even more accurate matching of digital images by manipulation at a later date.

Viewing such carefully presented image collections, perhaps made years apart on different sides of the globe, is a real pleasure. Many whole plant specimens are simply too large to be treated in this manner and need separate careful treatment. Try and use the same time of day with the cloud cover similar and the light coming from the same direction. Once again, the use of the same piece of grey card, if necessary on a separate exposure, will facilitate later colour matching on digital cameras.

Consistent results are the holy grail of image collections. With the use of standardised methods of lighting, this uniformity is greatly facilitated. The tent shown here on the right was used to take the picture of yellow rattle (*Rhinanthus minor*), above. It can be used in daylight, or with flash for greatest consistency.

# Close-ups and flower colours

A common problem with many close-up images of plants taken in the field is the intrusion of unnoticed but unsightly blades of grass or some other vegetation between the camera lens and the subject, or bright coloured highlights glowing out of focus in the background. When the camera has been set up on a tripod it is possible to shift the camera focus onto both areas and spot the offending objects before the exposure is made.

Some particular flower colours seem to defy an accurate colour rendition on film and to a rather lesser extent on digital cameras. The reasons behind this failing are complex, and stem from the way the colour image is created. With film there is little that can be done other than to change the type of film being used and compare the results. Different films have different responses to colours. On digital cameras image manipulation on a computer will normally more or less cure the problem, but it does depend upon your personal skill in the use of the software.

Large plant specimens viewed relatively close up in cramped conditions, such as trees in a dense forest, can be very difficult to photograph without excessive distortion. The required wide-angle lenses need careful control or your image will have trees which appear to curve unnaturally. The use of a spirit level on the camera will often help keep this within acceptable bounds, although the amount deemed acceptable is very much a matter of personal preference.

Many flowers will cause problems of correct colour rendition for both film and digital cameras. The plant species affected will vary according to what make of film or camera is used to record the image. Generally this colour shift is correctable with digital images but just occasionally it is too excessive. Overexposure or underexposure can also cause colour highlight or shadow shifts, even when the basic level of density is compensated for in the digital rendition. This can be seen in this pair of foxglove (*Digitalis purpurea*) images. The image to the right has been overexposed and has distorted colour balance while the one above is a more accurate representation of the flower.

Lighting, viewpoint and image size are all essential aspects to be studied before embarking on a time-lapse series, such as this one of daffodil (*Narcissus pseudonarcissus*) flowers. It is very easy to be caught out by a flower that opens up too large for the frame at a given working distance.

# Time-lapse recording

Perhaps because it is such an immediate medium, photography is only rarely used to its full potential to portray change over time. Time-lapse photography is a powerful scientific tool for monitoring change in environments, especially in relation to vegetation cover over months or years. Similar precautions to the matching of images in collections need to be incorporated into a carefully recorded procedure that will stay with the first images. In addition, data on the precise camera location (expressed as an eight figure grid reference) and colour balance information on the original image needs to be recorded. For pinpoint accuracy, you should drive a small post into the ground as a site marker so you can set up your tripod and camera at the exact spot on later visits. Notes on the purpose of the proposed image series and detailed descriptions of vegetation types will also be useful in any archive. In modern digital systems this data can all be linked together, even if

we do have to cross our fingers that it will still be around and accessible in fifty years time.

The title given to the botanical section of the Wildlife Photographer of the Year Competition – 'In Praise of Plants' – aptly describes a photographic style that has grown up around entries for the competition section. Some might feel this has a little too much of the 'Lord of the Rings' feel about it, but it has certainly encouraged an interest in the portrayal of plant communities as commanding scenic shots. The unwritten rule for such images seems to be to show no evidence of human effects on the landscape and an underlying drama to the lighting and landscape form. As a result, many of the pictures entered are taken in remote parts of the world and often reflect the photographers' pride in their national wilderness areas. This is a fine example where good creative photography can reflect a deep knowledge of, and personal feelings for, a subject.

# Plants in different climates

Like insects, plants, or at least bryophytes and lichens, can be found well into the polar regions. In these cold regions growth is static for most of the year but for the short period around midsummer it can be very rapid indeed. The snow vanishes and within days the tundra is green and dotted with flowers. This dramatic transformation is an ideal natural phenomenon lending itself to a series of beautiful images. Temperate regions have their own spectacular shows of colour each spring and autumn, such as the appearance early in the year of drifts of flowers like bluebells or daffodils and the reds, golds, yellows and other colours of autumn leaf fall, but these are less reliable and are less consistently reliable in the extent and beauty of their displays, with merely poor or average years as well as good ones. Blending the landscape background together with a specific plant interest is a frequently successful ploy for images of this kind.

Photographing tropical plants always presents problems, with harsh natural light being the chief one. It means that maintaining consistently well-lit subjects over a period of time is extremely difficult. Tropical forest vegetation grows in an uncontrolled riot and separating one species from another by eye can be a trial. Separating them photographically often takes many hours of searching out the right specimen. Many photographers have resorted to the plant collector's trick of separating off the leaves, flowers and fruit in a tasteful arrangement on a plain background. If you should try this method do remember to obtain permission to collect first and scrupulously observe any protective legislation. The approach is fine on its own as record but reveals no habitat information on the species. Blending the two approaches and accepting the constraints of both may hold the key. It is entirely possible to achieve this with modern digital techniques by holding all the separate image information in one poster-like file.

**Extreme cold requires special precautions to be taken to ensure cameras keep working. Batteries will often fail under such conditions and will need to be kept warm. Some manufacturers offer cold weather servicing which will be useful before such a trip. Concentration on the job in hand can be a practical problem under extreme conditions. Take extra care with camera settings and focus and do not rush yourself.**

# Reducing weight

Like many other experts, botanists may hit the field weighed down with kit. A comprehensively equipped camera case is the last thing they want to drag along, especially in the tropics. If the image requirement is more in the nature of a record than serious illustration, the little digital camera models will solve this problem admirably. They will produce a file size just large enough for report illustrations or even limited identifications. Being quick to use and light to carry, they can seem like a dream come true for making records of plants in the field.

The one problem some people find with them is one that relates to defects in their eyesight. All these little cameras have a small viewing screen in place of the traditional viewfinder. This means that you have to be able to focus your eyes alternately on the subject, some distance off, and then on the little screen a few inches from your eyes. This becomes very difficult or impossible for those who wear spectacles for both reading and distance vision unless they are wearing bifocal or varifocal glasses. The traditional single-lens reflex viewfinders got around this problem by installing extra little lenses in the viewfinder. These lenses could be adjusted to match one's eyesight. This is not possible with the screen-viewing method.

Above: It is always worth asking yourself what you are likely to do with an image and using the answer to help you decide just how you will shoot your subject. Is the shot a botanical study, or simply an image of a pleasing form? The picture of a bell orchid, top, has all the botanical requirements of a pleasing species record, while that of the African daisy (*Dimorphotheca aurantiaca*), below, contains considerably less information and, moreover, still has failings as a graphic or artistic shot.

Left: Spectacles steaming up frequently makes for problems for the photographer, especially in hot climates. Always have a dry lens cloth to hand and make sure that you have tested all optical systems with the glasses you will be wearing before you leave on a trip.

# Habitats

# Habitats

Setting aside the eye and skill of the individual, landscape photography has specialist technical requirements that set it rather apart from conventional wildlife photography. Most cameras in the right hands can produce very acceptable landscape images, but the really stunning images usually come from specialist pieces of kit such as panoramic cameras or designs allowing some adjustment to the lens axis. This adjustment is known as camera movement. The advantages that these cameras can give become apparent in the angle of view obtainable, the possible depth of field and the large film size or digital file that they will produce. Many specialist landscape cameras have built in spirit levels, but it is worth using a separate level on other models in order to avoid the horizon becoming tilted.

A picture of a landscape will normally have an angle of view that encompasses several miles of horizon. When this is reproduced as a small print the only recognisable feature will be the shape of the horizon. All the other detail will be so reduced in size as to become dots. Several methods have been used to overcome these drawbacks. To many people, the description 'landscape' essentially implies sunsets and horizons. To some extent this is an understandable assessment, as these features frequently form important parts of the images, but the nature of the intervening land can add so much more about the location and feel of the moment.

Control of camera movements will allow a crisp focus from inches in front of the camera right out to the horizon, and will finally overcome the 'ribbon of interest effect' that many poor landscapes suffer from by introducing foreground interest. If you cannot afford such specialist equipment much can still be done with conventional gear,

but be sure to use a tripod, and keep your exposures long so that you can benefit from the very small apertures that will result. The use of these small apertures will bring all the close detail into sharp focus. Remember to focus one-third of the way back between the nearest and furthest points that you need sharp in your image. As your lens is stopped down it will increase the area rendered sharp unequally outwards from this point, until the distant horizon and your closest point become sharp simultaneously. There is of course a limit to this, but it is surprising just how much you can pull into focus, especially with wide-angle lenses. To help produce large prints showing masses of fine detail, very-high-resolution film or a digital camera with a large chip and consequent high megapixel count will capture sufficient information.

Previous page: Mount Pyramid reflected in Lake Patricia, Jasper National Park, Alberta, Canada. Landscapes through the changing hours and seasons are the stuff that photographers dream about. Luck with the weather can play its part but mostly it is planning that is the key.

Above and below: Panoramic cameras will take in a wide sweep of countryside but the images they create need to be reproduced large in order to reveal all the detail they contain. Beware of flat lighting or large areas of blank sky, and be aware that distortion can be difficult to control.

## Wildscapes

The potential of wildlife landscapes is immense, but the difficulties are not to be underestimated. Overcoming the technical problems of focus and bringing some pertinent wildlife into shot within recognisable distance can be difficult to say the least. All the major migrations of large animals, from herds of Arctic caribou crossing the frozen tundra to the treks of vast numbers of wildebeest across the immense hot, dusty savannah plains of Africa, have been used successfully for this sort of image. To include smaller animals at a closer more personal level is considerably more difficult. Retaining instantly recognisable 'jizz' that indefinable blend of features that immediately sums up a particular species from what are minor features of the animal in question is more difficult still, but can turn a mundane image into a winner.

All photographers are always looking for that personal way of seeing things or a new angle or aspect on an old theme. Available-light night photography is an ignored field and landscapes by night even more so. Interestingly, this is an area that has to date not improved much with the change to digital image capture. Night-time light levels require long exposures, and digital imaging does not work very effectively under these circumstances. Indeed, many digital cameras have an electronic limit on the long exposure possibilities. The problem is caused by random electronic noise generating white dots in the image during the long exposures, so for the moment film is the better alternative for this sort of work. If you are prepared to take on the challenge, then nightscapes and starscapes could greatly extend the scope of your interest and produce exciting results.

As with all wildlife photography, wandering about aimlessly with a camera rarely produces results. The best approach requires thought and a clear knowledge of the effect that one is setting out to create. The image should already exist in the mind's eye. In this way it is possible to mentally run through locations, lighting conditions, weather and wildlife interest. Using a compass on the first visit to a location will allow you to predict the lighting at different times of day for any given viewpoint. Having mentally created the image, you then have a much better chance of actually getting the act together and being in the right place at approximately the right time. Many professional nature photographers are likely to agree that they have spent far more time waiting for light to change when photographing landscapes than on any other occasion.

Opposite: An insect such as this broad bodied chaser dragonfly (*Libellula depressa*) may be stunning in its own right but in its own environment it has a different visual effect, just as there is a difference between an insect in a collection and one observed in the field. Photographically this is a technical challenge, and the final presentation of the image usually has to be as a conventional isolated illustration.

Images that combine fine detail in a foreground with a sense of depth into wide landscapes can be impressive. They also convey much more about species than straight portraits ever can, as shown by these carrion crows (*Corvus corone*), right, and a Eurasian oystercatcher (*Haematopus ostralegus*), below.

## Shape and form

Finally, this is a type of photography that selects and extracts natural graphic forms and patterns and uses them as abstract imagery. Images of this sort frequently engender strong personal appreciation – or occasional dislike. Increasingly, such photographs are used enlarged and framed as artwork. Commercially they usually have little illustrative use and when used at all are seen as background images, often behind text or with smaller images set against them. Occasionally they have been used as the basis of pattern in the production of fabrics and wallpapers.

Training one's eyes to see naturally occurring shape and form is something that usually comes quite easily to most people with a reasonably well developed sense of design. Developing the technical mastery that can capture and intensify what the eye has seen is a further extension of the skill. A good way of learning to achieve this is to select a particular theme and then produce as many variations as

you can within a few hours. It is surprising how the single-minded concentration needed to achieve this, even over just a brief period, will improve the quality of your results. Looking for shape and form will improve the skills of most photographers; they have a strong tendency to spill over into other work and can provide the structure and continuity that leads to the formation of a personal style.

On the whole the subjects involved in shape-and-form work do not resent the photographer's presence and will normally be there for re-shoots days, months or even years later. One famous wildlife photographer has long been fascinated by a particular group of sinisterly formed birch trees growing on the shore of a remote sea loch in Scotland. This striking subject awaits his return to re-shoot a failed image from more than twenty years ago. Although this group of silent sentinels may have changed a little, the brooding pattern will still be there to capture as a haunting image.

Left: The pattern, form and atmosphere of a landscape or seascape can only be enhanced by the animals that live in it. The more the animal looks a part of the scene, even to the extent of almost melting into the background as a result of camouflage, the more likely you will be to achieve an interesting and aesthetically pleasing result that says much about the subject. In this image the impact of the common seal (*Phoca vitulina*) is subdued – and echoed – by the colour and pattern of the broken water. It is not a totally successful image but one that has potential to be re-shot to greater effect. Such 'good tries' should be regarded as personal memos for further work.

Opposite: A radio release was used for this rather different picture of an Atlantic puffin (*Fratercula arctica*). The wide-angle lens has allowed the inclusion of the misty seascape to enhance the image.

# Looking ahead

For individuals from the richer nations world travel opportunities are currently almost limitless. The effects of this travel should be seen as positive, for without the cash from tourism many of the best natural areas would have been developed several decades ago. However, this does not mean that everything in the garden is rosy far from it.

At a meeting with several friends last Christmas a discussion arose about the best places in the world to see various rare bird species. The phrases, 'you will need to hurry to see that one,' or, 'that may have gone now the area was being developed,' just kept being repeated. It was interesting to hear about the birds and that they are still there to be seen, but the underlying implications were very depressing. Most countries have powerful laws to protect their wildlife but in many places these are never enforced. Visitors to such places must be seen to obey local wildlife protection to the letter, if there is ever to be a hope that habitat destruction or wildlife exploitation will cease.

Whether you approach your chosen subjects as a photographer first or as a naturalist first, you will find the diversity of the natural world awe-inspiring. The technical challenges of the two approaches are quite different but when you manage to get them closely tied together the final results will greatly outshine either approach in isolation. Both pursuits are basically recording but together they can become a very fine art form in which style and content can give an almost limitless range of opportunities – enough to fill many lifetimes. With our wild planet fast becoming overpopulated, greatly tamed and indeed having its entire future put in jeopardy by climate change, it is more than ever necessary that the world as it is now is lovingly documented. There are many people out there who are unaware of, or oblivious to its complicated beauty. It is your task as a naturalist or photographer, or both, to raise that awareness.

This picture of a group of downy birches (*Betula pubescens*) is an old image – not in terms of this particular shot but in terms of the original idea. Few approaches are truly new in photography but this does not mean that an idea cannot be reworked or improved upon to great effect. Studying old photographs – and even old paintings – will often lead to successful new ideas and approaches to a theme.

# Glossary

Note: terms printed in **bold** type indicate other related glossary entries

**Ambient light** The light already present in a scene, excluding any source of light, such as that from a flash unit, introduced by the photographer.

**Ambient temperature** The temperature of an animal's surroundings, which may affect its degree of activity, especially with 'cold blooded' creatures, such as reptiles, amphibians and insects

**Aperture** An opening, usually adjustable, in the **lens** of a camera that controls the amount of light reaching the film or the image sensor of a digital camera. Setting the camera to a particular aperture has a major effect on depth of field as well as exposure. The setting is measured in the form of 'F numbers', which represent the **focal length** of the lens divided by the aperture diameter. The larger the F number, the smaller the aperture. See also **stop**.

**Auto-exposure** Or automatic exposure. System whereby the photo-electric cell measuring the light reaching the film or digital **chip** is linked to the **shutter** or **lens** aperture, and adjusts the exposure automatically.

**Available daylight** Existing natural light during daytime, without flash or any other artificial source.

**Available light** Method of taking photographs using just the existing low night photography light levels at night, without flash or any other artificial source introduced by the photographer.

**Break-beam system** Or beam-breaking system; device linked to the camera that enables the photographer to get an animal to effectively take its own picture by interrupting an infra-red beam and triggering the camera shutter.

**Camera speed** Refers to the shutter speed set on the camera at the time of exposure.

**Catchlight** The white highlight in the eye of an animal produced through reflection of the light source; adds life to the image.

**Chemical decay** As well as fading over time if exposed to light and being prone to attack by mould, stored film negatives and prints react with gases and other chemicals present in the atmosphere. Even when carefully stored in archival folders this degradation will proceed over long periods of time.

**Chip** Or imaging chip. The light-sensitive imaging sensor fixed at the **focal plane** of a digital camera, which takes the place of the film in a film camera. It consists of a grid of many microscopic light-sensitive **pixels**; each pixel measures the intensity of one of the three main primary colours, red, blue and green, or in the more recent X3 (triple-well) type, all three of these simultaneously, to collectively build up a dot-by-dot representation of the image. Each pixel produces a digital signal, and by converting these electronically into digital signals, the image can be recorded onto the camera's **memory chip.**

**Chip sensitivity** The equivalent in digital cameras to the ISO rating for **film speed**.

**Colour saturation** Highly saturated images have deep bright colours, low saturation images look pastel or even towards monochrome.

**Combination** Two or more images exposed on top of each other to make exposure one final image.

**Compact camera** A small, easily portable camera with the **shutter** mechanism incorporated into the **lens**.

**Compressed file** To save space on computer hard drives, CDs, DVDs and other digital storage systems, files can be compressed to a mere fraction of their original size. The downside is that the more an image is compressed, the greater the loss of image quality; although this does not matter for use on a website or even a small sized print, it does when printing at larger sizes.

**Daylight exposure** An exposure made using daylight as the source of lighting.

**Default setting** The setting of a parameter on the camera such as the film speed or **autofocus** setting that was chosen by the manufacturer and must be changed via a menu if you want to select another option.

**Depth of field** A measure of how much of a picture is in focus, from the nearest point where the image appears sharp to the farthest. Depth of field can be increased by using a smaller aperture, i.e. stopping down the lens. See also **aperture, stop**.

**Diaphragm** Or iris. Multi-bladed mechanism that opens and closes to control the amount of light passing through the lens. See also **aperture, stop**.

**Diffuser** Any device that uses material to scatter light so that it is softened and shadows appear less harsh; used especially with artificial light sources, materials used for diffusers include white cotton sheets, polystyrene or silver foil. Dust in the atmosphere and clouds may have a similar diffusing effect.

**Digiscoping** The recently developed art of attaching a compact digital camera to a telescope to enable one to take relatively large images of distant birds. Although one can simply hold the camera over the telescope eyepiece, it is far better to invest in a dedicated adaptor kit to attach camera and telescope together securely.

**Dupe** Short for 'duplicate'. A copy of a slide or negative.

**'Eight by ten'** A large size of film used in a large-format camera, loaded into the a special holder that is then inserted into the camera, one sheet at a time, in total darkness.

**Exposure** The amount of light used to create a photographic image: see also **auto-exposure** and **manual exposure**

**Extension tube** Sometimes called extension ring, and a useful device for close-up and **macro**-photography. It is a tube that fits between the lens attachment on the camera body and the camera **lens**, producing a greater distance between lens and film and thus enabling the lens to focus more closely and magnify the object more than would otherwise be possible. They come in slightly different lengths to produce different magnifications when used singly, in pairs or all three together (the latter producing a life-sized image with a standard lens). For producing larger-than-life images, extension bellows can be used.

**Field of view** The area of a scene which a particular lens and camera setting can record as an image.

**Fill-in flash** Flash used as a secondary light source, typically in daylight. As well as adding sparkle to an image taken on a relatively dull, overcast day, by boosting colours and contrast, for putting **catchlights** in the eye of a subject, and for softening and eliminating foreground shadows of backlit subjects.

**Film speed** The term used to describe the sensitivity of different film to light; a fast film requires less light to produce a correct exposure, while a slow film needs a good deal more (provided by opening the camera shutter for longer or using a larger aperture to open the **lens** wider . Film speed is measured nowadays using the ISO scale: films range from slow ones, ISO 25-64, faster ones, ISO 100-400, and very fast films, ISO 640-3200. The slower the film, the finer the grain and the more detail will be shown in the resulting image.

**Filter** A disc of transparent material that fits in front of a **lens** (or an artificial light source) and modifies the image or light in some way. Recently, the term has also come to be used for the many special effects designed to alter digital images using image-manipulation computer software.

**Flash exposure** An exposure made with flash as the source of light.

**Flash** Method of ensuring that the maximum output of light from the synchronisation flash unit coincides precisely with the time the **shutter** is completely open. The burst of light may last only 1/40,000th of a second.

**Flash tube** A glass tube filled with xenon gas which is ionised by an electric discharge to produce a brilliant flash of white light. Used in all photographic flashguns.

**Focal length** The distance, measured in mm, from the optical centre of a **lens** and its **focal point**. This gives an idea of the angle of view and magnification of the lens (or of a particular setting in a zoom lens).

**Focal plane** The flat surface in the camera on which the image of the subject is focused; it is where the film in a film camera or the imaging **chip** in a digital camera is sited.

**Focal point** The position where parallel lines of light entering a **lens** converge to a point.

**Format** Originally, referred to the size (height and width) and shape of the image recorded by a camera or to describe the camera itself, but now also describes the type of file used to store images digitally (see also **JPEG** and **TIFF**), which varies according to the resolution (degree of detail) as well as the image size.

**Greyscale** Chart made up of patches attached to a card, ranging in equal increments from white through a whole series of pale, mid and dark greys to blacks. Used for detecting contrast and colour changes in images.

**Hot shoe connector** Mounting system on a camera that incorporates an electrical contact for connecting a flashgun.

**Image cropping** Masking off or cutting unwanted edges of a film print or negative or of a digital image to produce a more pleasing design or to fit it into a smaller space when reproduced, e.g. in a book

**Infrared shutter** A system utilising invisible infrared light instead of a cable release to fire the camera shutter. release **Iris** See **diaphragm**.

**Jizz** The overall impression of a bird by an experienced birdwatcher, enabling him or her to identify it to species or group level from clues such as shape, size, behaviour, overall plumage pattern, even after only a momentary view when plumage details cannot be distinguished.

**JPEG** Type of digital image format; JPEG (short for Joint Photographic Experts Group) is the usual format used by most digital cameras.

**Large format** Film camera using sheet film measuring 5 x 4 inches or larger; uses sheets of film that have to be inserted into a special holder and loaded into the camera one at a time; used with very slow, extra fine grain film, this type of camera must be very accurately focused and kept very still to produce very fine detail.

**Lens** Photographic lenses do not consist of a single element but are arrangements of several glass or plastic 'elements' arranged in groups, that produce an image of the subject. Movement of one of the groups focuses the lens, and in a **zoom lens** alters the **focal length**.

**Lens hood** Truncated cone shaped device that attaches to the front of a **lens** to stop any stray light from outside the image area entering the lens so that flare (unwanted, unattractive highlights or over-softness of an image reducing contrast or creating a haze) is eliminated or minimised. Hoods should be designed for the lens being used, otherwise they may cut corners off the resulting picture if they are too deep, or give inadequate protection if too shallow.

**Lens mount** The part of a detachable camera **lens** for attaching it to the body of the camera; bayonet pins fitting into sockets on the camera provide electrical or mechanical

contacts to control the **aperture** of the lens from the camera.

**Macro** Adjective describing equipment and techniques for taking pictures at very close range to produce a bigger image, either life-size or larger (i.e., with a magnification ratio of 1:1 or greater).

**Macro telephoto** A lens designed to work at its optimum in the close up range, but giving telephoto working distances.

**Manual exposure** Method of setting the exposure for a shot by hand (compare with **auto-exposure**).

**Mechanical shutter** A mechanical method for releasing a shutter. A cable release.

**Medium-format** Term usually used to describe a range of cameras designed to take roll film of various different image formats, typically the 120 size but also 70mm and 220mm and various obsolete roll film sizes. Various camera models produce different image formats – usually 6 x 4.5 cm, 6 x 6 cm, and 6 x 7 cm. These would typically produce 15, 12 or 10 exposures from a roll of 120 film. The 220 film has double the length of the 120 type and produces twice as many exposures. Interchangeable backs on these cameras allow films of different types and formats to be used during a shoot.

**Megapixel** A million **pixels**.

**Memory chip/card** A device for storing images in digital form: small one in the camera or one in the form of a removable card that can store far more images). Some cards are known as memory sticks. The images can be read by the camera or on a memory card reader, which enables the uploading of images from the card onto a computer without involving the camera.

**Menu system** System appearing on a screen on the camera or in the viewfinder enabling one to see what camera settings are chosen and to change them.

**Micro-drive** Miniature hard drive used to store images in some digital cameras.

**Micro-switch** A device where a very small mechanical movement that will close an electrical contact.

**Modelling** Use of shadows to create the illusion of three-dimensional form in the final image.

**Modelling light** Feature available on some flashlights that uses a bright tungsten bulb to give a visual representation of the lighting the flash will provide when it is triggered.

**Motor drive** Motorised device within a camera that winds on the film and resets the **shutter** after each exposure; most types now also permit fast continuous shooting, taking several frames per second.

**Pixel** Short for 'picture element', a pixel is one of the many data points making up a digital image.

**Plate camera** Old-fashioned camera that instead of film uses glass (or sometimes metal) plates coated with light-sensitive emulsion to take pictures.

**Pneumatic shutter** See **mechanical shutter release**.

**Polarising filter** Or polarizer. **Filter** attached to a **lens** that, when rotated, allows through only light that vibrates in a single plane. Used to deepen the colour of the sky or other part of a picture and also to reduce the reflections from water or glass.

**Predictive autofocus** System that not only continually adjusts the focus automatically until the **shutter** is pressed, but also keeps adjusting it during the delay that occurs between pressing the shutter and the moment of its opening. This is a great aid in accurate focusing when tracking fast-moving subjects such as birds in flight, since it monitors the changing position of the subject and predicts where it will be for the next exposure.

**Random electronic** The phenomenon by which a digital camera produces white spots noise in an image during long exposures.

**Range-finding** A **focusing** method used on many cameras, usually employing an optical system consisting of a mirror, lens and prism. It displays two images seen from slightly different viewpoints; when the two are superimposed, the shot will be in focus.

**Reflex viewing** A viewfinder system utilising mirrors and/or prisms to look out through the lens that will expose the film or digital chip.

**Remote control** Device designed to trigger the camera **shutter** from a distance.

**Ring flash** A system of flash lighting that uses a flash tube in the form of a ring attached to the front of the camera **lens**. This produces even, shadow-free illumination all round and is particularly suited to close-up shots.

**Shutter** Camera mechanism for controlling the length of time that image-forming light is allowed to fall on the film or digital **chip**.

**Single-lens reflex** A single-lens reflex (often abbreviated to SLR) camera allows you to see through the camera **lens** as you look into the viewfinder. A reflex camera uses a system of mirrors to reflect the light that comes through the lens, and thus the image that it forms, onto a visible screen. This means that the image seen in the camera viewfinder is exactly the same as the image that will be recorded on the film or digital **chip**. Also, most reflex cameras show a high percentage of the image as it will be photographed (usually 80% or more, and in some cases 100%). The advantage of this system is that it provides the most accurate focusing and framing. Most direct view cameras suffer from parallax problems, which arise because the lens through which the eye is viewing the scene is separate from the lens that produces the photographic image, and does not give an accurate indication of the end result.

**Skylight filter** A combination of an amber coloured 'warm-up' **filter** and a UV **filter** that has the effect of both warming up the tone of a picture and reducing haze and any over-blue colour cast. They also have the bonus of protecting the vulnerable front end of a valuable **lens** from scratches and knocks.

**Slave flash** Flash system fitted with a 'slave' device that triggers one flash unit to fire at precisely the same moment as one or more others.

**Specific gravity** Or relative density. The ratio of the density of a substance to that of water.

**Standard** The **focal length** of a **lens** that is approximately the same length **focal-length** as the diagonal of the area of the image it produces, which is roughly the central in-focus view seen by the normal human eye. For a **35mm camera**, a 50mm lens is usually regarded as the standard lens.

**Stop** A unit of exposure. To 'stop down' a **lens** means to reduce its aperture, i.e. increase its F-number. Reducing by a single stop means that one has halved the light that reaches the film or digital **chip**. Similarly, increasing by a single stop involves doubling the light that enters. The distance between each standard aperture setting (f/4, f/5.6. f/8, etc.) is known as a full stop. See also **aperture, F-number**.

**Telephoto lens** Or simply telephoto. A long-focal length **lens**, which will produce magnified images of distant subjects with a narrow **field of view**.

**35mm** The usual film size used in **single-lens reflex** and **compact** film cameras.

**TIFF** Short for Tagged Image File Format. Digital image format that can record maximum available detail from an image. Although the file size is large, it can be reduced if required (as when storing on a hard drive, CD or DVD, or when sending as an attachment) using lossless compression without losing information.

**Time-lapse** Technique in which shots are taken of the same subject at regular photography intervals so as to capture an event that occurs over a long time, such as the opening of a flower or a leaf from a bud, taking hours, or changes in vegetation cover over a period of months or even years.

**Transparency** Often abbreviated to 'trannie'. A slide taken using reversal (or slide) film that, after being processed, produces a positive image.

**Ultraviolet filter** Or UV **filter**; a filter placed over a **lens** that absorbs ultraviolet (UV) radiation; it has the effect of making an image clearer, especially those taken in mountains or aquatic landscapes.

**Wide-angle lens** A **lens** with a distinctly greater angle of view compared with a **standard focal length** lens.

**Zoom lens** Or simply zoom. **Lens** that has a continuously variable **focal length** and a variable angle of view over a particular range, e.g. 35–80 mm or 28–120 mm, at any given focus and **aperture**. It provides a range of magnifications and fields of view in a single lens, thus obviating the need to carry several separate fixed focal-length ones.

# Index

Page numbers in **bold** refer to illustration captions.

# Picture credits

pp. 4-5 © John Shaw/NHPA

pp. 6-7 © Lorne Gill

p. 8 © Frank Greenaway

p. 9 © Chris Knights/Ardea.com

pp. 10-11 © Frank Greenaway

pp. 12-13 © Jonathan & Angela Scott/NHPA

p. 14 © Frank Greenaway

p. 15 (t) © Frank Greenaway; (b) © Steve Hopkin/Ardea.com

p. 16-17 © Ferrero Labat/Ardea.com

p. 18-19 © Frank Greenaway

p. 21 © Nigel J. Dennis/NHPA

pp. 22-3 © Frank Greenaway

p. 24-5 © Martin Harvey/NHPA

p. 28-9 © Frank Greenaway

pp. 34-5 © Bill Coster/NHPA

pp. 36-7 © Frank Greenaway

pp. 38-9 © Helen Cowdy/NHMPL

pp. 40-1 © Frank Greenaway

pp. 42-3 © Ellen Goff/NHMPL

pp. 44-5 © Frank Greenaway

pp. 46-7 © David Tipling/NHMPL

pp. 48-9 © Phil Hurst/NHMPL

pp. 50-7 © Frank Greenaway

p. 58 © Phil Hurst/NHMPL

p. 59 © Frank Greenaway

p. 60 © Stefan Meyers/Ardea.com

p. 61 © Phil Hurst/NHMPL

p. 62-5 © Frank Greenaway

pp. 66-7 © Nigel J. Dennis/NHPA

p. 68 © Thomas Dressler/Ardea.com

pp. 69-70 © Frank Greenaway

p. 71 (t) © Ann & Steve Toon/NHPA; (b) © Phil Hurst/NHMPL

p. 72 © Joe Blossom/NHPA

p. 73 (t) © Kelly-Mooney Photography/CORBIS; (b) © Bettmann/CORBIS

p. 75-89 © Frank Greenaway

pp. 90-1 © M. Watson/Ardea.com

p. 92 © Frank Greenaway

p. 93 © NHMPL

pp. 94-9 © Frank Greenaway

p. 100 © Martin Harvey/NHPA

p. 101 © Ken Lucas/Ardea.com

p. 102 (t) Ian Walker/NHMPL; (b) © Mark Bowler/NHPA

p. 103 © Joanna Van Gruisen/Ardea.com

pp. 104-5 © Janos Jurka/NHMPL

p. 106 © Steve Hopkin/Ardea.com

p. 107 © Phil Hurst/NHMPL

p. 108-15 © Frank Greenaway

p. 116 © Paul van Gaalen/Ardea.com

p. 117 © Frank Greenaway

p. 118 © Pascal Goetgheluck/Ardea.com

p. 119 © Francois Gohier/Ardea.com

pp. 120-21 © Frank Greenaway

pp. 122-23 © Valerie Taylor/Ardea.com

p. 124 © John Clegg/Ardea.com

pp. 125-28 © Frank Greenaway

p. 129 © Phil Hurst/NHMPL

pp. 130-31 © Valerie Taylor/Ardea.com

p. 131 © Ernie James/NHPA

pp. 132-33 © NHMPL

pp. 134-35 © Jens-Peter Laub/Ardea.com

pp. 136-41 © Frank Greenaway

pp. 142-43 © Simon Colmer/NHPA

p. 144 © Janos Jurka/NHMPL

p. 145 (t) © Nick Garbutt/NHPA; (m) © Jonathan Ayres/NHMPL; (b) © NHMPL

pp. 146-47 © Francois Gohier/Ardea.com

pp. 148-53 © Frank Greenaway

p. 154 © R. Sorensen & J. Olsen/NHPA

NHMPL: Natural History Museum Picture Library, *www.nhm.ac.uk/piclib*

Every effort has been made to contact and accurately credit all copyright holders. If we have been unsuccessful, we apologise and welcome corrections for future editions and reprints.